THE "THINKING AND DOING" OF NATIONAL SECURITY – A PROPOSAL FOR THE PRESIDENT

by
Bob Polk

Order this book online at www.trafford.com
or email orders@trafford.com

Most Trafford titles are also available at major online book retailers.

Printed in Victoria, BC, Canada.

ISBN: 978-1-4269-2620-4 (sc)
ISBN: 978-1-4269-2621-1 (hc)

Library of Congress Control Number: 2010900473

*Our mission is to efficiently provide the world's finest, most comprehensive book publishing
service, enabling every author to experience success. To find out how to publish your book, your
way, and have it available worldwide, visit us online at www.trafford.com*

Trafford rev. 3/11/10

 www.trafford.com

North America and international
toll-free: 1 888 232 4444 (USA and Canada)
phone: 250 383 6864 ♦ fax: 812 355 4082

CONTENTS

Acknowledgments/Dedication

I would like to dedicate this to my two kids, Kristina and Thomas, and their mother Karole, for the years of sacrifice and support that goes into a profession of service.

   I would also like to send special thanks to the Honorable James R. Locher III, Dr. Sheila Ronis, Dan Langberg, Caroline Earle, Len Hawley and John Tsagronis for being inspirational friends and contributing experts.

About the Author

Robert Polk has served in various senior level planning and execution management positions both in and out of government. Today, he remains a Senior Adjunct Research Member and Consultant at the Institute for Defense Analyses in Washington, D.C., where his ongoing experience helping develop planning and execution capacity in several U.S. departments continues to provide valuable insights.

He recently completed three years as Senior Advisor, Strategic Planner, Deputy Issue Team Lead, and cofounding member of the Project on National Security Reform (PNSR), which continues to work on developing reform initiatives for the national security system beyond planning and execution management, including systemic redesigns across the sectors of human capital, knowledge and resource management. While at PNSR, Bob was able to observe and participate with some of the best minds in Washington on the issues and potential solution sets of the day.

Preceding these experiences was Bob's twenty-year military career as both a front-line combat infantry officer and senior civil-military strategist for major Army and multiservice commands, serving across the international spectrum from Thailand to Japan to Bosnia to Germany and Iraq.

The latter posting included many months as the Co-Creator and Co-Director of the Office of Policy Planning to the United Nations-sanctioned Coalition Provisional Authority Ambassador, L. Paul Bremer, in the early days of Operation Iraqi Freedom.

Preceding this, Bob served as the Director of Plans for the original U.S. civil-military coordination team going into Baghdad, called the Office of Reconstruction and Humanitarian Assistance, led by retired Lieutenant General Jay Garner.

Bob's military career included work as a senior strategist with the Office of the Secretary of Defense's U.S. Interagency Transition Planning Team and Afghanistan Reach-Back Office.

Bob also served as a U.S. Army Strategic Fellow to the U.S. Department of State at its Foreign Service Institute, working to organize department level gaming sessions on complex national and international issues, from the original 2002 game on intervening in Iraq to the U.S. strategic positioning for rejoining the U.N.'s Commission on Human Rights. Leading to this assignment was his two-year tour of duty as a Lead Senior Strategic Planner for the U.S. Army I Corps, which culminated years of service in numerous and varied military command and staff assignments around the world.

Bob holds three masters degrees: a Master of Military Arts and Science in Operational Theory and Strategic Planning from the United States Army's premier School of Advanced Military Studies, a Master of Arts in National Security and Strategic Studies from the United States Naval War College, and a Master of Science in General Administration from Central Michigan University.

Bob received his Bachelor of Science in General Engineering from the United States Military Academy in 1985.

He is a native of South Arkansas.

Foreword

I woke to the sound of the first salvo of rockets lifting off from their pod set up on the back of a donkey cart only three hundred yards away.

SWIIIIOOOOOOSH. KABAM!

Again. SWIIIIOOOOOOOOSH. KABAM!

The sounds were essentially the same as the volleys continued, but the aim of our intended killers was nearing where I was sitting.

I was sitting on the edge of a bed in a darkened room in a dank and musty abandoned hotel in the middle of a U.S. compound in a country not my own. It had only recently become my latest home away from home after months spent in various quarters around the vicinity.

My roommate awoke, a veteran of many decades of similar situations. There we both sat in our sleeping shorts, counting silently as if we knew this was a six-shooter and we would be safe if ...

Again, SWIIIIOOOOOOOSH, KABAM!

Still we sat, hands by our sides, as if waiting for our turn for the bathroom; as if preoccupied and waiting to return to sleep.

I had been shot at before, but this was my first time being at the epicenter of a terrorist attack. My military background had desensitized me to an extent. I had always expected danger and/or death, but in an almost clichéd manner - I could not help think, 'Not this way. Not without a chance to fight back. And not in my skivvies.'

In that same moment, I accepted the fate that might come in the very next instant if a rocket were to also penetrate my window, as it had undoubtedly already done just a few feet down the hallway. I would not dive for cover. I would accept. The only words I remember were me saying to my colleague, "This doesn't sound good. There are going to be some folks hurt this time around," and his reply of, "Yep."

Forty rockets later, in what may have been thirty seconds of real time on the watch, the immediate situation concluded with the usual after-sounds of stray crackling bits of residual concrete finding its final resting place. My room had been spared – no direct hit.

Only hours earlier we had been awakened by two rockets impaling themselves only meters above, outside our window, but this attack seemed to have been directed from the other side of the building. Twenty-seven of the forty munitions would make it through twenty-seven windows of my civilian and military colleagues. Remarkably, a military peer of mine would be the attack's only fatality. Yes, smoke or dust was in the air, in the hallways. Yes, I could hear the sounds of folks making their way rather calmly out of their rooms toward the staircases. Yes, from the sixteenth floor I could hear the hallway guards stationed twenty-four hours a day for just such a drill taking charge of the situation as best they could.

I knew I was headed for another evacuation and immediately a long day of work without access to all my stuff. My reaction was … to take one last shower.

You don't know where this took place. It doesn't matter. You or I could have been anywhere. In fact, it has been anywhere and everywhere for some time – terrorism, that is. In my moment, not the first and not the last, I found a kinship with all those who suffer the indignity of such a cowardly act. I also found my own sense of self in those times – a calm, a peace followed by a period of some regret for not being more heroic in some unknown way, and a wee bit of paranoia at the thought of more such attacks.

This opening story captures in my mind both a moment I reaffirmed the difficulty in choosing viable national security endeavors that make sense, and my moment of decision to address this at the source, at least in America, where policy is made.

Yet this book is not about terrorism, policies or policymakers who work on any particular national security issue. It is about the process that underpins those national security policymakers in deciding whether, when, where and how to address any issue, including putting us all in crazy places around the world with rockets pointed at our windows – or tanks.

Yes, I said it. This is a book about process – the process of the thinking and doing of national security, and it is my belief that a proper, flexible system approach can scale and apply to any national mission, foreign or domestic. My aim is to present you with just such an approach.

To be certain, some of you are no longer reading this book, this sentence. Process folks around the world are currently serving several back-to-back life sentences in the minds of the world's doers. These doers see process as a euphemism for tail chasing, leading to an inevitable 'paralysis of analysis' by bureaucrats who conflate 'thinking' as 'doing.' And yet, we all have our talents. I guess I am just the latest glutton for punishment.

In truth, thinking and doing are two sides of the same coin of national security, joined by process. One can't exist without the other and neither can survive alone or together without process. It is like water to the human body. It is time to see the system as a whole and not as an either/or. To all my brothers and sisters who like doing more than thinking or who fancy themselves as perfectly balanced experts in both, I salute you. I only ask for your indulgence. My intent is to add, not to take away; to heal, not make worse; to simplify, not complicate. In the end, you be the judge.

But first, a disclaimer. I believe that before we understand how something works, we must first take that step to simply think it or dream it. There is plenty in my proposal that needs to be worked out. I acknowledge this as a scientist might when he or she presents a working hypothesis in a scholarly journal to his or her peers. I too want to stimulate the discussion by first presenting a dream, even if not a completed one. I have done enough work to believe in its workability, but I am admittedly banking on its plausibility more than its undeniableness. Human genome sequencing was thought of once before anyone actually knew how it could be done. Most thought it impossible in even the next hundred years, but it took less than twenty to achieve once the dream was out there.

All 'hows' are 'what ifs' at some earlier stage. None of this is said to dissuade or evade, only to invite your critiques in the spirit of collaborative discovery rather than in the spirit of competition.

Finally, I don't expect this book or the processes proposed in it to solve 'world hunger.' Moreover, in the hands of the wrong person, any new system can be as useless as the one it proposes to replace. And in the end, this country will continue to face a never-ending stream of national security issues that may never be fully resolved. So, why even try to worry about the system that underpins all this? Well in my mind it is simply about getting an advantage. A bad system can only make things worse. A good system gives us a better chance. In particular, my proposal just might help keep America in the driver's seat a little while longer with just enough foresight, context, and wherewithal about ourselves to stay one step ahead of the competition. I will leave it to the American people as to whether that advantage will ultimately be used for good or bad. As for the system that creates this advantage, I say it is worth a try.

I thank you for your time and attention, and I do look forward to your feedback.

Part I: Introduction

I have a difficult task ahead of me. I need to expose you to a set of proposals which, if properly improved upon and adopted, would make the president's job of integrating the national methods (ways) and resources (means) to support his/her aims (ends) 'better.' To do this, I feel an obligation to follow some logic that will make this easy to understand. Additionally, I feel an obligation to make this enjoyable to help you remember what I propose. Let me start with logic, followed by enjoyable.

The logic begins as follows: The world is complex and getting more so, and the president's staff and his Cabinet are struggling to get their daily jobs done. They are both either too busy or overwhelmed and they are hopelessly arranged both structurally and skill-wise to do the very basic for us all – the thinking and doing of national security. Certainly parts of the Cabinet and parts of the president's staff are doing their jobs quite well, but they are challenged mightily to do them well together as a team. Additionally, since it is the Cabinet that actually does the doing in the U.S. government, no matter what reforms take place 'above' the department level, they will be hollow if they aren't matched with the new department capacities to keep up.

The solution is not adding new tasks to cover more area or to add more staff to cover more area. It is adding new services from what I call planning and execution management teams to the existing overwhelmed organizations of the government. I am not talking about czar teams either. (Incidentally, the proliferation of these is the best example I know of an indictment of the current system.) I believe we need to take the burdens of the existing organizations down quite a few notches while offering the correct targeted and talented services directly to the parts of the existing system of the government as it needs it. If done correctly, the existing system can get back into its more traditional lanes with more time to do its job. This translates to more time devoted to the thinking and the doing at both the National Security Council (NSC) level for the president and the department level for the rest of us. Oh yes, Congress will love this too because a less stressed executive translates to a better partner to the legislature. In my proposal, Congress will also be able to actually participate more directly in this less stressed executive system. I will explain all this as we go along.

At the time of this writing, I have to admit that there are some good folks in Washington trying to work all this out – just not enough and with almost zero real support from either the White House or Congress. Champions for process reforms are hard to come by when the headlines remain dominated by citizen issues such as health care, global warming, shutting down Guantanamo Bay, economic woes and two wars. For example, who in Peoria really cares about how the NSC is organized? Consequently, what politician cares about anything his constituents don't care about? I told you this wouldn't be easy.

Yes, this book is about stuff that folks in Kansas or Nevada or right here in Virginia don't really care about. And perhaps they shouldn't ... but someone should.

In particular, this book is about the thinking and doing, or as I like to say in Washington bureaucratic speak, the planning and execution management, of national security. It has been my long observation, with few exceptions in very narrow niche sectors of the Washington crowd, that these two ideas are usually mentioned in separate company and not as they should be, as two sides of the same coin. I will try to right this injustice with this book.

No one has ever seriously presented:

A single, fully inclusive approach to both planning and execution involving all the various actors from across the breadth of government and commercial sectors working seamlessly together in a continuing narrative of both top-down and bottom-up efforts; capable of handling any issue of national security, from the strategic to the tactical, both at home and abroad in the near, mid and long-term, and in both geographical and functional dimensions; where the end result is the integration of the national ways (methods) supported by the national means (resources) to support the many national ends (purposeful aims) in the context of its environments.

I say this coming as a once cofounding and full-time member of the most serious recent effort in many years in Washington to recommend just such a system – the Project on National Security Reform (PNSR). In my opinion, the PNSR has not yet achieved its intended reforms primarily for one reason – it still struggles to find a compelling single narrative in all its recommendations. Instead, and with no disrespect to my many talented colleagues, it continues to present a series of complex and overlapping narratives in several seminal areas of national security. In the area of planning and execution management, it is only just now beginning to see the full spectrum of connections.

To me it is simple. In complex systems there is usually a chief narrative supported by contributing narratives. I submit that for the U.S. national security system, the chief narrative is the end-to-end process of both the thinking (assessments, policy, strategy, planning, feedback, etc.) and the doing (operations/implementation/execution) as one in the context of its environments. I would only add my colleague Patti Benner's definition of what national security is at root: "Anything that affects the viability or vitality of the nation." Period.

National security and its system is, then, as widely and narrowly encompassing as one chooses (I choose widely). You can now begin to see why I propose a system approach called (for my Washington bureaucratic colleagues) a "National Security Planning and Execution Management System" – a system addressing both the thinking and the doing of national security as equals.

And now, for a bit of the enjoyable.

Dream Sequence 1 (Everything is a System):

The phone rang on a Monday evening. The proposal was simple – go to the country of Econistan, assess the situation, then put together a team to restore order to the country before things get out of hand and devolve into a greater, more complex challenge.

I had the president's personal invitation and authority. I would be an envoy – that venerable, squishy title that strikes fear in the heart of mainline bureaucrats because it is, in effect, the proverbial blank check to make mischief in Washington, but with none of the proper authority or resources to actually do more.

That said, I would leave in the morning for a five-day, whirlwind tour of the affected areas. I would be back in Washington on the sixth day and, by the seventh ... well, you know how the story goes. I had a lot to do in a short time.

The country didn't seem as stressed as the mission implied, but I found certain aspects of the situation that could use our attention. I began to see clearly what was in front of me and I put a call in to an old friend to be my Chief of Staff. The role came easily to her and she immediately went to work lining up necessary presentations for required decisions upon my return to D.C. Within days we had assembled the perfect team – twenty-two in all – and we were set to arrive in-country for our official transition into our lead role in ten days.

Upon touchdown, Econistan's presidential reception party whisked me away from my staff to the presidential palace, where I assured our host that we had a plan. The situation was well in hand. With a longer-than-usual squeeze, he shook my hand with a deep and sincere hope in his eye, and I was off.

My life experiences, both in the military and in the wider interagency world, had prepared me well for what lay ahead. The team was forming and the reports coming in seemed rather manageable. My first communiqué to the President of the United States was full of the usual ups and downs, but clearly the advances made in interagency operations since those crazy days in Iraq and Afghanistan over a decade ago were comforting.

The report on that clear day in November, however, gave me my first pause. Why hadn't we seen this coming? More importantly now, what do we do about it? The unrest in the outer parts of the rural regions was not good and getting worse. We had come in with a plan with exactly the right three priorities, and we had doggedly pursued them, as one should. These priorities were well thought through by my team of experts. Why were these folks in the rural areas now seemingly at odds with what was clearly the right and best set of decisions we could make? Never mind; time heals all things.

My drive over to the presidential palace would not be as pleasant as the last. I had been summoned in the midst of my admitted stalling for over two months. My analyses showed that the situation was coming unglued in spite of picking the <u>correct</u> three priorities. We just didn't see the other factors at play – we hadn't taken the time. Our forward field offices were all under rebel control and now the entire U.S. government mission was in jeopardy. By the time I reached the palace the reports were arriving at an increasing pace. The end was near. What had I forgotten from all my training as a national security professional since this system had been instituted eight years earlier, and how had all of us allowed this to happen? The car came to a stop and the door opened ....

<u>The Main Lesson:</u> Without a systems approach, there can be no systems solution, and so many aspects of both the problems underneath the problems and the various potential solution sets can never be revealed.

<u>In our story I had learned the following:</u>

- Nothing is as simple as it seems. There are always hidden connections.

- There is never a <u>correct</u> way. There are only the ways that are best based on the situation.

- Persistence in the face of overwhelming evidence pointing to other systemic issues is a recipe for disaster.

- Finally, had I approached the problem as a system rather than a single or even two-dimensional situation, I might have seen the signs of unrest at an earlier moment, when its mitigation was possible.

PART II: HOW EXACTLY MIGHT A NATIONAL SECURITY PLANNING AND EXECUTION MANAGEMENT SYSTEM LOOK AND FEEL?

To get us all playing from the same sheet of music, you may wish to consider my assumptions underpinning the proposals on the following pages. If you buy in to these, then we may have a good relationship forming. If you don't ... well, I hope you do. If these assumptions aren't yours going into this discussion together, then the proposals I make will seem equally uncertain to your senses. Again, I can only ask for your indulgence at this early stage. Perhaps if you give them a chance, we can both come to a better set of assumptions and solutions by the time this discussion concludes (long after this book is published).

Here they are, my going-in assumptions that prompted me to write this book. I would be happy to hear your feedback. Remember, this proposal is a work-in-progress, primarily about process and, for now, primarily about the U.S. national level processes for national security. It may not play well in Peoria, but I trust it will be for their greater good in the end.

Assumption #1: You have actually heard this one already, but it bears repeating. No matter the form (people, structure, etc.) or function (tasks, goals, etc.) added, my assumption is that neither the NSC nor the Cabinet alone, nor in any combination together, can handle the process of bringing the greatest coherency and coordination across the United States in all the national security issues areas likely to face us throughout the 21st century. The Cabinet can't command their peers. They need someone 'above' them to do this for them. And neither the NSC nor the Cabinet can possibly embody all by themselves:

A single, fully inclusive approach to both planning and execution involving all the various actors from across the breadth of government and commercial sectors working seamlessly together in a continuing narrative of both top-down and bottom-up efforts; capable of handling any issue of national security, from the strategic to the tactical, both at home and abroad in the near, mid and long-term, and in both geographical and functional dimensions; where the end result is the integration of the national ways (methods) supported by the national means (resources) to support the many national ends (purposeful aims) in the context of its environments.

If this exists today, someone please point it out to me.

Assumption #2: You've heard this too, but they say learning comes through repetition. The Cabinet, NSC and the president all need help, and my assumption is that more staff isn't the answer. What they all need is a more effective thinking and doing management service. This service should be provided to both the Cabinet and the NSC to relieve them from trying to do it all by themselves and, therefore, doing nothing extremely well, and to allow each to stay focused on their respective primary roles of government. In the case of the NSC, that primary role might be to remain focused on helping develop the president's purposeful aims/ends and ensuring the Cabinet members have what they need to be successful in carrying out these aims/ends. In the case of the Cabinet, it might be to carry out the 'doing' of government on behalf of the president and the American people.

The NSC can't provide the services that I listed in Assumption #1 through their current Interagency Coordination Committees, Deputies Committee, Principles Committee process alone – not enough time, attention, skill sets; and did I say time ... and skill sets? The Cabinet cannot either. They all need the professional services I listed in Assumption #1, provided to them, in part, through a new organization within the Executive Office of the President.

In this sense, my Washington, D.C., colleagues will understand that a reasonable analogy is the planning and execution management service provided by the Joint Staff in the Pentagon both <u>up</u> to the Office of the Secretary of Defense and <u>down</u> to the five services (Army, Air Force, Navy, Marine Corps, Coast Guard). Think of it as taking the heavy lifting of some thinking and coordination off the backs of the Office of the Secretary of Defense and the services so they can each stay focused on their primary roles. Providing this service also provides a bridging function between these two communities when necessary, as they integrate the department's ways and means to support the ends selected by the department secretary.

To expand the analogy, the Department of Defense (DoD) organizations that manage and cut across the services to do the bulk of the military work around the globe are the ten Combatant Commanders. In this case, the Joint Staff still provides a certain part of the overall thinking and coordination function. The Combatant Commanders are not so much up or down, but this time <u>out</u> from the Joint Staff. So, in the end, the Joint Staff performs functions up, down and out within the DoD to keep the machinery working and to allow all to stay in their primary roles. Again, this is similar to the less successful executive branch efforts to develop organizations that manage and cut across the various departments.

Finally, to complete the analogy, the DoD's Planning, Programming, Budgeting, Execution System is a worthy example of the kind of ends, ways, means integration system that should underpin the U.S. national security system, as it currently underpins the Joint Staff, the Office of the Secretary of Defense and Combatant Commander system in the thinking and doing of military business. It is far from perfect but it is a good attempt worth studying.

What I will propose for the national security system is not a Joint Staff or Planning, Programming, Budgeting, Execution System per se, but a unique variation of sorts.

<u>Assumption #3:</u> As alluded to already, my assumption is that the much-vaunted czars, or other uber-organizations such as the National Counterterrorism Center, Director of National Intelligence, and so forth, can not be considered as feasible alternatives nor additions until due diligence has been taken to care for and adjust the primal or foundational NSC/Cabinet system first. Such organizations are each designed to offer the executive branch its own smallish version of a Combatant Commander. These are organizations in addition to the departments intended to manage and cut across all the other departments, usually on behalf of a single issue area, unlike the much more robust Combatant Commander model, which manages many issues from the five DoD services and Office of the Secretary of Defense at once.

These executive branch uber-organizations have arisen over the decades as a symptom of the foundational problems underlying the existing executive branch. Rather than rebuild the foundation, we have proliferated band-aid fixes. If, after adjusting the foundation, such offices are still necessary to provide focused planning and execution management at a lower level, then they will also find the services of my proposed bridge organization critical to their success, just as the Combatant Commanders and the Office of the Secretary of Defense could not well survive without a Joint Staff.

Dream Sequence 2 (Ends):

My head was swimming as I arrived in Econistan. Everything seemed to be in place but I had a certain nagging feeling that something wasn't quite as it should be. The meeting with the president seemed to confirm my inner suspicions as he shook my hand goodbye.

As my convoy proceeded back to our new headquarters, I called ahead to talk to Kristina, my Chief of Staff, an experienced national security professional and one of the first out of the National Security Professional Corps Academies commissioned in 2012. She agreed with my sense of unease, and the staff was waiting for me upon arrival.

"I want you all to understand that I realize we have put our hearts and souls into this plan," I began. "We have turned over every stone, and these three priorities we've settled on make sense as the right priorities ... but I have to also tell you that, as a fan of systems approaches, I am not sure we have crossed the finish line just yet. I would like you all, led by the Chief of Staff, to consider whether there are other factors we may have overlooked."

The briefing went well, and my sense of understanding about the problems and their causes reached a never-before-seen standard of excellence.

I immediately consulted with Econistan's president for his government's view on whether the rural areas might be a source of unexpected unrest. With no disagreement, we proceeded to implement new programs affecting the people directly through our field offices.

This time, a nagging intuition had led me to a proper and complete analysis of the situation as a system. We now had a multitiered approach to the situation at hand, and that night I rested easy.

The morning reports on the numbers two and three field offices being overrun with casualties had to be a mistake. Our plan had specifically taken the systems approach and determined all the parts that could pose a problem. With such an approach, how could I be responsible for what could not be foreseen?

I gave instructions requesting immediate relief, and this time the U.S. President's office was calling to ask why the President of Econistan was complaining about our ineffective strategy.

I was due to be replaced at the end of the month. The official word was that I had successfully made it to my planned transition point, but the media was already spreading rumors of my firing. The casualties had mounted in the interim.

As I looked out my airplane window, I turned everything over in my mind. Yes, rebel leaders had expressed a desire to communicate with me about their demands, but my mission was not to help them but to help the people in the rural regions. To hell with the rebel leaders; they were rendered moot by my policies of outreach to the people.

I could not understand how I had miscalculated what was truly the center of gravity. I had taken my eye off the ball, or perhaps I had never really seen it in the first place.

I drifted off to sleep to the drone of the military transport engines evacuating my staff and me.

The Main Lesson: Without a clear-eyed vision of some end, there can be no effective execution toward that outcome.

In our story, I had learned the following:

- Even with a complete understanding of the parts and how they all fit into the whole, as systems thinking will allow, I had failed to recognize the true focus for the overall system or mission. The focal point was not one group of people over another but the stability of the country in a way that could ensure conflict would not arise in the long term. This adjustment of the ends, or the end state conditions that must be set before we could declare our mission truly effective, was my undoing. I had such a narrow approach to my systems thinking that I left no room for the rebel leaders and their followers to find a compromised approach. Consequently, the rebel leaders took sides rather than consider working with my team. I had driven them toward my Achilles' heel. My ends had been misdiagnosed and my tactical systems approach could not make up for this strategic myopia.

PART III: KEY DESIRED SYSTEM ATTRIBUTES

If I previously left you with my top assumptions that will underpin my proposals for a new systems approach to the thinking and doing of national security, let me here offer my take on what would constitute the key attributes of such a system. As the reader, you may use this information to evaluate whether my proposal includes these or you may again wish to take issue with my list and seek to modify it or add your own. Consider these as starters:

1. The planning and execution of national security should be thought of and managed as a single holistic system.

2. The Executive and Legislative branches of government should act as full partners in achieving this purpose and in overseeing the system's components that make up the whole.

3. The National Security Planning and Execution Management system should fundamentally be about the entire end-to-end process of integrating national Ways (national methods or conduct or courses of action) with the national Means (national public and commercial resources where possible, including Congressional and gubernatorial support) to support the achievement of the national Ends (national vision and aims set by the president).

4. The National Security Planning and Execution Management system should include both a formal and informal system of decision-making for the president and other key leaders.

5. The process of decision-making in this management system must have transparent steps, tools and membership that either eliminate or significantly reduce individual or group cognitive biases.

6. Classification barriers must be reduced among the team of participants in the system. The err should be on the side of risking some of the heretofore passive security regime in America at the expense of generating unprecedented offensive momentum created as a result of an all-knowing whole of the national ends, ways and means team approach.

7. The National Security Planning and Execution Management system should be able to see and make sense of the entire world in contexts, especially noting the weak signals on the horizon before they become a problem.

8. The National Security Planning and Execution Management 'doing' side of the system should transcend peer or Cabinet level competition to get things done.

9. The National Security Planning and Execution Management 'thinking' side of the system should separate out (and value) long-term thinkers and short-term thinkers with appropriate incentives and interactions between the two in order to keep both halves aware of the whole and, therefore, relevant to each other.

10. The National Security Planning and Execution Management system should emphasize agility and decentralized execution through the use of living core U.S. government capabilities, structures, leadership and processes (both physical and mental) able to quickly assimilate and

manage (in both thinking and doing) contributing surge capabilities, structures, leadership and processes from across the spectrum of private and public sectors as needed.

11. All the participants in the National Security Planning and Execution Management system should be supported by an easily scalable classified and unclassified standardized backbone of common information architecture.

12. At its root, the National Security Planning and Execution Management system should answer continuously: What is driving the national security system now and into the future (Ends)? How will it proceed now and into that future (Ways)? What is the United States willing to spend on that future (Means)?

Dream Sequence 3 (Ways):

The President of Econistan had his staff prepared this time. They each took turns outlining the specific angles on the surplus of problems plaguing their own ability to make progress toward lasting stability. We were all in agreement that the conflict drivers were sometimes subtle but that dignity and respect would need to be a hallmark of the end game across the various actors. Each had their own way and we had to find a process for incorporating all of them.

Kristina and her deputy, Thomas, also had prepared a series of presentations and we achieved unanimity on our focus and our priorities, specifically to deliver the same amount of relief supplies to both the rebel leaders and the local farmers. The rebel leaders were given a chance to coordinate their plans into alignment with ours and we began a process of deploying our field teams to monitor the situation.

I was convinced that we had finally arrived at a sustainable course of action to bring about our aims in concert with the systems analysis of all the affected actors.

Our plan to push our field offices out into the field was implemented with great speed. We had identified the need to ensure that relief supplies were getting through and so we were positioning ourselves accordingly. I had specifically chosen to have the relief supplies go in by truck rather than helicopter because of the fear and damage these machines imposed on the surrounding people, crops and primitive dwelling structures, along with the dust and confusion that ensued. Furthermore, supply rations were in effect and such fuel consumption was not a luxury we could afford.

The first supply trucks left and returned on time and the plan began to take on a rhythm. For certain there were setbacks, but I could distinctly remember the moment when I realized that the vision of our ends we had coupled to this way, or method, of achieving that vision was in perfect harmony. I was proud, perhaps too proud.

We all understood that the tribal areas had been drawn in the sand with blood over the centuries, and we knew the road networks were an historical bone of contention. In the latter part of the last century, these roads, built by other less compromising foreign influences, had inscribed their own sense of order on top of these ancient divides. We listened as reports came in that our plan was beginning to receive some resistance as our convoys crossed these boundaries, stirring the emotions and inflaming resentment. There was evidently an order to this world not apparent to Western eyes. The deserts had their ways, but we had our mission and an agreed-upon plan.

I had only taken a slight liberty to make arrangements to drive rather than fly over these boundaries. How could I have known the inflammatory nature of such a benign but logistically sensible decision? Yes, the convoys could be managed better – routes rerouted, etc. – and yes, in some instances helicopters might be the better choice to avoid some of the more obstinate tribal concerns. But the people must understand my situation as well. I had a job to get done and, while the democratic process has its merits, in crises, some shortcuts are necessary.

My convoy was just on the outskirts of the town as these thoughts concluded in my mind. By my actions with my very own convoy, I had made the bold statement I had intended. We had demonstrated our resolve to be both strong enough to adjust our plans and methods of implementation of those plans, but we had also drawn our own line in the sand on just how much we were willing to be pushed around. At some point, our authority had to be asserted.

I woke up in the hospital with my driver lying in the adjacent bed. The doctors were in motion and, as I regained consciousness, I felt the urge to move closer to my driver to see what was happening. My urge was overcome by a growing sense of my own situation. My legs were immobilized. I could not tell the extent of my injuries – my condition was not apparent because my concern was across the room. For what seemed like hours but was only minutes in reality, my driver had struggled to survive, but to no avail.

I strained to bear my guilt. I had been determined to pick the right ways to accomplish our ends but I was not prepared to shift or to compromise on those ways. The mission was not a complete failure but, as I would soon learn, my time in-country was over. Eventually, compromises would be made and the tribal leaders would reestablish their authority. With these concessions, the mission would continue, but only after great personal cost, all because I could not see the error of our ways.

The Main Lesson: Without implementing the proper ways integrated throughout the evolving process of both planning and execution, there can be no effective end accomplishment.

In our story, I had learned the following:
- The ways, or methods, of a plan can never be approved without a clear-eyed understanding of whether they will or will not support the ends intended. In this case, one way was not good for every situation. I had refused to consider evolving or changing and analyzing other options.
- There are usually multiple ways to address a single end. Not all are as good as the next and each must be analyzed for their cost/benefit. Additionally, what starts off looking like a best option may evolve into a bad option over time as the environment shapes it.
- Most ways should be considered variations from a base concept that can move and adapt at a moment's notice.
- Never get wedded to a way. Be flexible to the signs of when the environment will no longer sustain the chosen course of action.
- To be flexible, build structures or methods that are flexible, such as having both helicopters and trucks in the mix, giving you lots of options.
- To be flexible, build most implementation ways on a core and surge concept where the base capabilities are well known and simple, such as field office teams to which surge elements can add to those core capabilities as needed, such as more or fewer trucks or helicopters depending on the situation.

PART IV: SCOPE OF THE PROPOSED MANAGEMENT SYSTEM

My proposed National Security Planning and Execution Management system would belong to the entirety of national level actors in the United States, but includes chiefly the Executive Office of the President, state executive branches, federal departments and agencies, various appointed Presidential Issue Teams (a PNSR term, and an organizational proposal in contrast to czars and envoys), and various executive and legislative advisory and oversight organizations in the 'interagency space' (a term coined by the Honorable James Locher III, Executive Director of the Project on National Security Reform. It refers to that space between the president and U.S. departments, but does not necessarily include the space between the departments themselves. This space extends, in theory, beyond the Beltway).

The overall system would be managed by a newly proposed Director for National Security (DNS), a position also proposed by the PNSR in its 2008 report to Congress, "Forging a New Shield." This new position would in no way interfere with the authority of Cabinet secretaries or the informal system processes used by them and the inner circle of presidential advisors, staff and other policy makers and influencers. However, with a new formal planning and execution management system architecture in place in the Executive Office of the President, the president and his/her interagency constituents would finally have a single home for the joining together of all in the all-important collaborative planning process in lieu of the lesser important creation of the perfect plan by a few.

I have given you my going-in assumptions that drove my concern to write this book. I then offered a list of planning and execution management system attributes that I believe would ensure success. Now there has to be a new overall paradigm (beyond assumptions and attributes) for national security in order for a new Planning and Execution Management system to take root and function properly. The following proposes a set of system imperatives that, if taken as a whole and continuously utilized, will represent a new paradigm in how the national security system could function compared to the way it does today. These were developed during 2007 and 2008 in collaboration with my PNSR colleagues Dr. Sheila Ronis, Patti Benner and Dan Langberg. The system must be:

1. Perceptive in Nature – The new National Security System must have an ability to identify that which could affect the viability and vitality of the U.S. nation state (governmental and nongovernmental; foreign and domestic) in order to ensure that no potential national security threat or opportunity in the entire global and universal domain, no matter how remote, is ever overlooked. Here the proverbial 'Butterfly Effect' comes to mind.

"In 1969 Edward Lorenz, the famed meteorologist and Chaos Theory proponent, introduced the concept now known as the 'Butterfly Effect' when he posed the famous question: 'Does the flap of a butterfly's wings in Brazil set off a tornado in Texas?' The Butterfly Effect theory describes the phenomenon of how small variations in a dynamic system can subsequently cause larger and more complex variations over the long term." – Hezi Moore. http://virtualization.sys-con.com/node/997105.

The point is that we want a system that can detect these earlier variations before they become unmanageable trends. This first imperative asserts, then, that future perceiving must far outstrip current conventions in both ways and means to achieve its ultimate purpose of keeping the system informed.

Current examples of where this matters today: Failure to track and understand the impact of the shift in international and national demographics, especially as it pertains to youth and unemployment, may lead to major miscalculations of their negative implications. Failure to recognize the full range of climate change and the opportunities to mitigate its effects before it is too late. Education standards slipping to the point of the United States dropping out of the top fifty countries in the world for the critical disciplines.

Future examples of where this might matter: Not understanding the nature of technology transfers from the United States to others, or from our adversaries to other actors, until it is too late. Not understanding the vulnerabilities of over-reliance or under-reliance on certain technologies before it is too late. Not understanding cultural and religious shifts until the polarization is too great. Not understanding the nature of the threats to geosynchronous space and other property regions in the larger solar system before it is too late. Not reacting to vulnerabilities in health trends and threats before it is too late.

2. <u>Natural and Agile in Behavior</u> – The new National Security System must have the ability to act naturalistically with core and surge capacities across all disciplines in the national security community both in and beyond government. By natural, I mean acting in ways that do not always presume to impose nonorganic, non-native or unnatural behaviors onto native or natural actors and their systems within their own environments.

Historically, humanity has been in constant dissonance with nature as it tries to tame what it cannot. Building cities and dams is not what I mean. In the long run, nature always dominates unless unnatural efforts are constantly maintained. The future environment may comply even less with such demands as the interactions between the increasing number of actors and systems continue to grow into a dense fusion of interactivity. Finding the right flow in the patterns will become more efficient than trying to prescribe the perfectly correct program against the grain. Core and surge methods of behavior are the natural counterbalance to this world of increased uncertainty, complexity and even chaos. Core and surge presumes limited ways and means to apply to these natural environments and so seeks a balance easily flowing from one incarnation of ways and means into another to address these evolving patterns of environmental change. The core refers to those ways and means that may address the known and knowable domains. They may be of a more permanent nature. The surge refers to those ways and means that may address the unknown and unknowable as they evolve into the knowable and known over time. They may be of a less permanent nature. Core and Surge have roots in both theory and practice. Many experts recommend core and surge behaviors as the preferred approach for responding with openness and agility to any environmental factor.

"A robust U.S. response capability needs surge capacities, expertise and resources that can flow immediately, unencumbered by bureaucratic constraints." – 'On the Brink: Weak States and US National Security,' The Center for Global Development, (p.4).

In the end, a core and surge behavior embraced widely throughout the entirety of the U.S. government would represent a true paradigm shift. If implemented fully across the depth of its intent, it would create a tectonic change whose seismic activity would send shock waves across the whole of government. No agency and no function would escape its effects. In its wake would be strewn the remnants of our 20th century system and in its place would stand a true 21st and, indeed, 22nd century capability.

Luckily, we have experience to look to as harbingers of this possibility. In the Department of Defense, it is called 'Modularity,' and the Marine Corps is a living testament to its success. In business, it is called 'Mass Customization,' and nobody does it better than the Toyota Motor Corporation. Both systems are designed to prioritize core capabilities against core requirements while maintaining standby capabilities for lesser priority requirements as they may arise. Core and surge behaviors require adjustments in context, sensing, prioritization and acting, and self-awareness in all its component parts, coupled to a behavior that drives the system into action and keeps it on keel.

Current examples of where this matters today: The Marine Corps long ago realized that it could be given any mission in any part of the world at any time. Faced with such a daunting challenge, it adopted a modular approach to the application of its ways and means. First, it realized that its most basic and flexible unit was the marine itself. Consequently, today, its most basic core capability is simply a brigade of marines.

Secondly, the Marines realized that in order for this basic unit to quickly suit up for any mission operating in any environment within just a few hours, it must be able to quickly add any number of additional experts and equipment that might be peculiar to that mission and that environment. This became the Marines' surge capability. The core units are more permanently drilled and maintained, while the more specialized experts are given less attention until called upon. In this way, the Marines are ready for anything, anytime, while applying their limited resources in the most efficient and responsible manner possible.

Future examples of where this might matter: The United States may be forced to apply the strength of the whole of government to respond to more than one humanitarian and/or pre- and post-conflict crisis on multiple fronts (both foreign and domestic) simultaneously. To that end, it would be difficult to maintain several generic, fully manned composite U.S. government Response Corps to send out to each crisis. It would be more efficient to maintain several fully manned composite nuclei of core capabilities and then apply additional specialized experts on a more temporary basis tailored to each particular event as needed. Consider Figure 1 below as a concept worth debate.

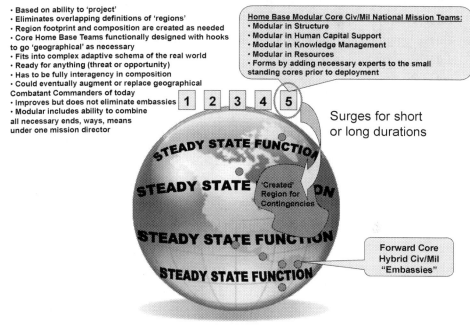

A National Modular Contingency Team Concept

• Based on ability to 'project'
• Eliminates overlapping definitions of 'regions'
• Region footprint and composition are created as needed
• Core Home Base Teams functionally designed with hooks to go 'geographical' as necessary
• Fits into complex adaptive schema of the real world
• Ready for anything (threat or opportunity)
• Has to be fully interagency in composition
• Could eventually augment or replace geographical Combatant Commanders of today
• Improves but does not eliminate embassies
• Modular includes ability to combine all necessary ends, ways, means under one mission director

Home Base Modular Core Civ/Mil National Mission Teams:
• Modular in Structure
• Modular in Human Capital Support
• Modular in Knowledge Management
• Modular in Resources
• Forms by adding necessary experts to the small standing cores prior to deployment

1 2 3 4 5

Surges for short or long durations

STEADY STATE FUNCTION

STEADY STATE 'Created' Region for Contingencies ON

STEADY STATE FUNCTION

STEADY STATE FUNCTION

Forward Core Hybrid Civ/Mil "Embassies"

Figure 1

3. <u>Selective in Behavior</u> – The new National Security System must have a method to exercise whole-of-government judgment to prioritize which global contextual factors, among the many it may sense, the whole of government will address and in what order. Understanding that no system can act equally on all that it perceives, a system needs a clear and responsive method of making sense of its priorities.

Current examples of where this matters today: The National Security Council and the Homeland Security Council are two bodies looking in different directions but tapping into the same governmental capital to address their own priorities. These often compete for the same overall pools of funding and personnel. The Obama administration did consider this in a presidentially directed study in 2009 and decided, as a result, to combine the two staffs while keeping the two councils of senior officials (advisors to the president) intact (primarily as a compromise to state and local pressure). But this arrangement is proving to be problematic as the two councils continue to seek the necessary care and feeding from the now one staff. So, each staff directorate in the NSC now has two separate councils to support. This is another example of a recipe for confusion and overloading of the already meager NSC staff, making selective behavior a near impossibility. From the tired NSC staff perspective, they now have twice as many priorities as before.

Of even greater concern is the fact that over the past several decades, the U.S. government has grown to include hundreds of departments, agencies, boards and commissions, all ostensibly reporting directly to the president. There exists no single venue where this diversity of individual or organizational interests is vetted and prioritized and then put into operation coherently across the whole of government. Moreover, there is no coherency to the myriad of executive and legislative funding trails supporting these individual priorities should they be determined anyway. Again, selective behavior is lost in the grind.

Future examples of where this might matter: When confronted with the numberless future internal and external influences that will create both threats and opportunities, system workarounds and adding staff without creating new functions will no longer do. Framing the implications flowing from the evolving environment will require a robust crosscutting fusion capability as never seen before.

A National Assessment, Visioning and Integration Center of some sort could provide a solution to this challenge. Such a fusion and coordination center would sit above the departments but below the NSC inside the Executive Office of the President to help make sense of the world and suggest whole-of-government and whole-of-nation options for how to interact with it, much like the Joint Staff does for the Office of the Secretary of Defense and the Combatant Commanders.

4. Decentralized in Execution – The new National Security System must have a method of bringing the greatest amount of awareness, judgment and decision-making closer to the point of action, so that action and resources are working together seamlessly in a more timely fashion with the least bureaucratic friction.

This imperative aims to minimize the compunction for perfect clarity leading to prescriptive, centralized approaches from the top, and instead focuses on facilitating the emergence of meaning to guide all the members of the system to act more in loosely coupled harmony rather than in tight and perfect synchronicity. Other imperatives, such as naturalistic and agile behaviors, for example, can only work if empowered by this decentralized approach to thinking and doing. Furthermore, reliance on 'higher' slows the response at the points of need, creating opportunities for other unforeseen threats to emerge in the confusion and time gap required for constant consultation between and amongst the layers.

Flatter decentralized organizational dynamics help eliminate this. While this imperative acknowledges that differing situations, from steady state to crisis, may demand variations of the decentralized approach, its basic qualities should prevail in each.

Yet there is a huge caveat to this imperative. Too many confuse decentralization with hand-offs and abdication. In fact, for decentralized behaviors to work organizationally, the central or higher components of the system must work equally hard at setting the proper environments for the outer or lower subordinate parts to operate on their own. For example, the sole reason the DoD exists, in operational terms, is to make the point of the spear work. Continuing this metaphor, if the pointy end is the Joint Task Force, the shaft is the combination of the Combatant Commander, the Joint Staff and the Office of the Secretary of Defense. All of these higher parts exist to make the front-line Joint Task Force successful at operating as it sees fit with limited drag on its decentralized efforts. Consequently, each of these layers has multiple roles in making that Joint Task Force successful. Some of these roles are decisional, some are advisory, some are technical, some are logistical, some are administrative (such as training the force) and some are financial (The Joint Task Force doesn't have to worry about money in the strategic sense – it isn't formed unless it has the requisite resources for the job). It is sheer folly, as we can see, to suggest or presume that the Joint Task Force is simply kicked out the door to act decentralized all on its own. It still requires a team to set those decentralized conditions as a team.

In a civilian illustration, a Presidential Issue Team could not hope to function in a decentralized fashion unless it knew that many of its essential support functions, like policy formulation, higher strategy-making, funding and other resources, were taken care of for it. It could not operate successfully if it were continually fighting this rear entanglement of raising financial and political capital for its work. Other layers of bureaucracy must fight these battles on a continual basis so that the front-line team can be freed to operate most effectively in a decentralized manner. This is why a National Assessment, Visioning and Integration Center must be considered in order to provide these supporting functions to such civilian teams that the overwhelmed NSC and Cabinet cannot.

Current examples of where this matters today: The Marine Corps could not act with its core and surge ability across the globe in multiple scenarios simultaneously without the other services, the Joint Staff and the Office of the Secretary of Defense. Neither could U.S. ambassadors nor United States Agency for International Development (USAID) teams around the globe operate effectively if their wider departments didn't have their backs.

Future examples of where this might matter: The Marines and overseas ambassadors will increasingly have to join with whole-of-government and other national partners as one team rather than separate entities to address a nation's threats and opportunities together, both abroad and at home. This will require an unprecedented acceptance and adoption of this basic imperative across the whole of government. Moreover, the proverbial 5,000-mile screwdrivers must be permanently shelved in favor of a new planning and execution management system that fosters the necessary support and collaboration from the home base to decentralized executors in the field without all the drag. Technologies will initially both help and hinder this as layers between home base, national and field actors will increasingly seem to disappear, unlocking both the desire for supervisors to meddle below their calling and actors in the field to run independently. A compromise will emerge as the concept of collaboration evolves.

NOTE: To some, the thought of decentralization may seem to run counter to the idea of being 'operational' in that it is very hard for a higher organization to be fully operational at one level but then allow the next lower level to be fully operational too. It seems as if there may be a contradiction.

Let's unwind this a bit, and to do this you will have to accept a definition I propose. In my definition, being operational is the ability to match funds (because money drives everything in the end) directly to actions with as little interference from outside actors along the way. Therefore, how operational any organization is can be measured by the number and complexity of layers between the thinking about (deciding) what to 'do' and the application of resources to support the 'doing'. For example, if an organization requires eighteen bureaucratic steps from decision to the application of funds to support the decision, then it has a quantifiable 'operational-ness' to it. The fewer the steps, the more operational that organization is. The more steps, the less operational. Therefore, every organization is operational along a spectrum from a more to a lesser degree, including the current NSC. The current NSC is on the lesser operational end of the spectrum today because it requires multiple complex steps (often out of its control) between its decisions and getting actions funded from across the government. So by my definition, it would be accurate to say that the NSC is somewhat operational in that it does have an ability to at least influence Cabinet funding priorities for its approved actions. The staff of the NSC would like to be much more operational in that it would have its own funding to direct actions as it please with no layers of checks and balances, but the law and the Constitution have made this impossible in all but the most exceptional cases.

This measure of how operational a person or organization is applies to whether an organization is acting in a centralized or decentralized manner. It makes no difference, in my mind at least, the measure remains valid and it is wrong to assume that how operational an organization is would necessarily affect how decentralized it may be in execution. Every level in the chain of thinking and doing may be operational to the degree it wishes and still provide the 'space' for the next lower level to operate decentralized in its own thinking and doing as long as each level stays in its own lanes or within appropriate boundaries. For example, a different legislatively and judicially approved NSC could be operational at the strategic level in that it could match strategic decisions directly to strategic resources (from a presidential contingency fund, for example) but an ambassador could still have all the decentralized authority to match country-level resources to his/her decisions at the country level as he/she sees fit. Both decentralized capabilities can coexist easily.

5. <u>Comprehensive in Ability</u> – The new National Security System must have the ability to map and mobilize whole-of-government, whole-of-nation and, eventually, whole-of-global capacities that exist to address national security priorities as required. To operate as a partner in this comprehensive arena, the United States must know with what it has to act. This also means that methods chosen must not limit themselves to U.S. government assets alone to address problems that will increasingly require all the tools of the entire nation and its partners around the globe.

To address this first point, the U.S. government will have to map all its classified and unclassified capabilities and put these capabilities into master databases that can be used in a myriad of ways for planning and execution management. However, the mapping of those capabilities is only a first step. To many, the resources of the National Security System are confined only to those that are explicitly owned by the government. Yet, as our first assumption states, we can no longer think in such limited terms.

The viability and vitality of the nation depends on the interactions and collaboration of the entire national, international, global and sometimes-universal domain, not just what it can muster inside the U.S. government. The larger outer environmental contexts do not care whether we here in America have this or that type of government or concept of living, working and playing. The global context does not act only according to our U.S. habits and requirements. It acts as it wishes for its own interests in ways that are often nongovernmental and perhaps non-American, both politically and socially, and so requires equally asymmetric collaborations for us all to be successful. To think otherwise is to miss the point behind the first assumption that the U.S. National Security System is only a subset of a larger global system that is largely beyond its ability to control.

Relatively recent examples of where this matters today: The Coalition Provisional Authority in Iraq was an exercise in how not to muster American power. Its ad-hoc and inexperienced cadre (and I was one of them) struggled to bring the whole of government together to make meaningful progress in a timely manner. By contrast, the mobilization in World War II across the entire national base, and the Marshall Plan that followed, demonstrated an ability to map and mobilize to historic success in measures never seen before or since.

Future examples of where this might matter: Global climate change, international mitigation of demographic shifts, global competition under the polar caps and into space, and continued international support to reduce and eventually eliminate tensions between cultures will increasingly demand such mobilization of U.S. and international comprehensive capabilities to dwarf even the Marshall Plan.

6. <u>Transcendent in Authority</u> – The new National Security System's ways must transcend, when necessary, stovepiped departments, agencies and Congressional committees in order to manage interagency activities with the commensurate authority (fiscal and otherwise) to take thinking and doing from the highest all the way through to the lowest point of execution. This means that some form of enforceable transcendence 'above' the sole interests of the individual sub-system components is necessary to achieve actions for the common good.

Current examples of where this matters today: The Office of Management and Budget, the Office of Personnel Management, the National Counterterrorism Center, and the Office of the Coordinator for Reconstruction and Stabilization in the Department of State are examples of cross-agency teaming for national budgeting, U.S. government personnel management, countering terrorism and nation building – functional areas that demand horizontal integration. Some of these organizations must rely on peers to voluntarily staff their ranks and comply with their recommendations. Peer relationships, however, can never fully accomplish these tasks even with strong lead-agency approaches. These uber-organizations have, to varying degrees, achieved some success by residing their limited authorities 'above' the departmental squabbles, but they are all struggling against the tide of peer noncompliance. True success in this endeavor can only be accomplished by an organization when its fiscal authority to become operational across all necessary participating partners matches its political authority.

Future examples of where this might matter: Grand Policy, Strategy, Cross-Agency Planning and Interagency Team Execution are rarely successful unless participation is mandatory and all manner of processes remain free from stultifying competition and infighting. Currently there exists no grand venue for such processes to take place that easily and seamlessly harmonizes all the participating partners across the U.S. government in a neutral place. A National Assessment, Visioning and Integration Center working in coordination with the National Security Council could take on such tasks by facilitating national level planning and execution management functions from an office placed 'above' any department but 'below' all national policy decision-making of the president, his/her staff and Cabinet. This Center would also perform the task of maintaining greater continuity in all such functions across changing administrations, led by apolitical leaders appointed for longer durations.

7. Integrated Across Seams – The new National Security System must be able to transcend, reduce or eliminate vulnerable strategic seams festering between aging paradigms that insist on continuing to draw clear and unambiguous distinctions between such categories as foreign

and domestic, civilian and military, public and private, governmental and nongovernmental, combatant and noncombatant, Department of Defense and the rest, etc., and replace them with distinct national security approaches incorporating more responsible and comprehensive ways. These traditional physical and mental boundaries are being stretched beyond their elasticity. The ensuing gaps create seams that offer strategic vulnerabilities to those who would take advantage. These must be mitigated or eliminated altogether with new paradigms that accept grey and overlapping qualities where others today see only black and white or sharp, hard edges.

This imperative is rooted in practice. There is no shortage of examples, from health scares to terrorism, the impact of the Internet on education, or the commercial sector thinking locally while acting globally to advance this idea that seams between and among some of our most venerable paradigms is fast approaching a new era of fuzziness or blurring in their distinctions. Consider that foreign and domestic as two distinct categories has guided Western thought since the nation-state was born worldwide. Could it be that the Venn diagram sets of what is purely domestic and what is foreign are increasingly overlapping to expose a growing lack of distinction between the two?

"We have taken a broad view of national security. In the new era, sharp distinctions between 'foreign' and 'domestic' no longer apply ... If the structures and processes of the U.S. government stand still amid a world of change, the United States will lose its capacity to shape history, and will instead be shaped by it." – U.S. Commission on National Security in the 21st century, (p. viii).

Clearly there will remain some distinctions between peculiar aspects of each of these domains, but, as stated earlier, it is folly to presume that future actors, trends, issues, events, etc., in the global or even domestic arenas will ever see these distinctions the way we do today. We have to evolve.

Relatively recent examples of where this matters today: For years the five services of the Department of Defense maintained separate but equal approaches to military operations. The seams between them were many and, in retrospect, the cause of great inefficiencies and, arguably, lost lives. The traditions were difficult to overcome, but the Goldwater- Nichols Act of 1986 did what many believed impossible – it created a culture of blended planning and execution with an ability to enforce it. Moreover, as already noted, the debate continues on the idea of ridding the National Security System of two security councils, Homeland and National (with the current decision only to blend the staffs but not the senior councils). With global threats increasingly moving between these domains, many believe the two separate councils have created a vulnerable seam ready for exploitation. The solution may be to bring the two together as one. (Here, I will even go as far as to suggest using a new word I made up to help us describe that which applies to both foreign and domestic as 'Fordestic'. It may seem silly at first, but perhaps new words like this might help us all move beyond some of the current bifurcated thinking and doing on such matters.)

Future examples of where this might matter: As global economic and technological forces increasingly blur the distinctions between how and where governmental and private sectors accrue their power in support of society, the nation will require unprecedented cooperation between the two. Once feared, this blending will be met with acceptance and understanding as the concept of whole-of-nation is truly born. (NOTE: This must include a top-down designed, bottom-up implemented federation of a whole-of-government knowledge management system to provide the vehicle upon which the understanding necessary to plug these seams will ride.)

8. <u>Balanced in Composition</u> – The new National Security System must ensure a renewed U.S. government civilian capacity to act (leadership, authority, roles and responsibilities) with unambiguous control of the totality of U.S. government actions (military or otherwise) with unbroken continuity at the national, regional, international and field

levels throughout the spectrum of security situations, without a break or a hand-off to the military. This imperative is posited as central to any possible vision of successful reform across the entire spectrum of planning and execution. There can no longer exist an 'us and them' in national security. There is only 'we.'

In the reformed milieu of the future, empowered civilian leaders must emerge capable of prosecuting to the fullest extent their responsibility to represent what is best about America into the field, regardless of the risks involved. This means unprecedented conceptualizations of a new non-Department of Defense government civilian leadership with corresponding authority to make decisions and vector resources on behalf of the entire U.S. government across and throughout the entire spectrum of planning and execution of any mission, from the national level out to the field.

This belief is born of the assumption that the U.S. government's current civilian authority to make decisions and vector resources in the field, overseas in particular, have waned in recent crises almost to the point of extinction. There are many reasons for this absence, not the least of which is the decades-long ascendancy of the professional U.S. military as the chief widget in our presidents' national security toolbox. For a number of well-intentioned reasons, the Department of Defense has created a presence that pervades foreign operations with a capacity far outstripping that of any other U.S. department or agency.

Reinvigorating the government's civilian roles would have two additional positive effects. In my estimation, a renewed civilian capacity would help reconnect the American people more unambiguously to their civilian foreign policymakers and policies in more tangible and accountable ways. Also, a more robust civilian leadership capacity would reduce the number of 'transition points' between it and the military around the world – points of responsibility that should never have been relinquished by civilians to the military in the first place. Eliminating such transitions, or hand-off points, by retaining responsibilities firmly and continuously in the hands of civilians would be a major triumph of efficiency and a development welcomed by a redefined and refocused interagency machine. This would include combat operations. Civilians would not direct or design the manner of operations, but they would approve the intent (which includes the articulation of the endstate conditions) at all levels.

This level of involvement is important because the civilian is always responsible for the outcome of any operation, military or otherwise. If the civilian is going to get the blame, the civilian should get the authority to shape the mission at all levels. Moreover, the future of conflict is such that civilian effects will remain not only central but causal to the ultimate success of any combat response, no matter the size, intensity or duration.

In sum, the future roles and responsibilities of government civilians vis-à-vis the defense juggernaut must be at the center of our reform efforts in education, training, human capital selection, organizational design and leadership. Consider former senator and current U.S. Secretary of State Hillary Clinton's statement on this issue:

"We don't have enough civilian capacity to manage pre- and post-crisis situations. The world has changed, but our civilian institutions and preparation for public service has not kept up." – Senator Hillary Clinton in a speech to the Council on Foreign Relations, October 31, 2006.

Current examples of where this matters today: The creation of a new U.S. African Command, complete with a robust and integrated civilian interagency staff component, is more evidence of the trajectory for blurring the distinctions between national security servants, whether from the Department of Defense or any other department/agency. While a useful incremental step, all the issues of leadership and authority reform as proposed here will not be resolved by this one progression of the U.S. African Command.

Future examples of where this might matter: As the nation continues its critical global engagement with partners around the world, the traditional relationship between the Department of Defense and the 'rest' of the civilian interagency will undoubtedly evolve into a more holistic and balanced arrangement. This will force a softer line between the two, even while the military component of the DoD may remain more efficiently distinct.

Non-DoD civilian leadership, however, may evolve to exercise unbroken continuity, including new civilians who have been educated and trained in both domains as never before. In such a cultural domain, civilian-led National Regional Commissioners may replace the venerable Combatant Commanders to augment the many country ambassadors. These civilian-led organizations may operate off a whole-of-government core and surge capability able to quickly respond and reload as needed for a myriad of national tasks.

9. <u>Streamlined in Accountability</u> – The new National Security System must have robust and effective Congressional and other oversight over the new 'transcendent' domains 'above' the individual departments and committees to enable the preceding system imperatives to work unfettered yet responsibly on behalf of the American people. This imperative addresses the fundamental need to remain Constitutional at all times as reform takes its new footing in the 21st century. Accountability is the people's connection to the process and so represents an essential and immutable imperative of any final system adopted.

Current examples of where this matters today: Billions of dollars remain unaccounted for in Iraq's reconstruction efforts. Unfortunately, the majority of observers have taken the wrong lesson from this experience. Most believe that the solution next time is greater oversight with no consideration for how this should occur. Traditional oversight could stymie efforts in the field and would be in violation of our previously proposed system imperative of being decentralized in execution. The proper lesson is to achieve this all-important oversight without creating intrusion into the timeliness or effectiveness of operations in the field.

Future examples of where this might matter: As information technology levels the playing fields around the globe, greater authority for matching strategic capital to action in the field will be in increased demand. Nimble oversight will remain crucial as a proper check on a system increasingly forced to make strategic decisions in minutes rather than hours to support a core and surge paradigm. Congressional interagency affairs committees will need to build institutional abilities to streamline their financial support mechanisms to the executive branch. A National Assessment, Visioning and Integration Center (NAVIC) would provide a partial answer, with its high and early oversight council mechanisms built into the system of both planning and execution management.

Dream Sequence 4 (Means):

The president himself seemed pleased this time as he shook my hand. I had briefed him on the progress of our planning in Econistan and he was satisfied that we had identified thoroughly what was driving the potential for conflict. In fact, he asked his staff to work with us on learning more about, and providing additional information as needed for, our analysis. The idea of bringing rebel leaders into the tent to speak with local leaders under a forum that made sense and protected everyone's dignity and equities had worked.

The plan was no longer just my plan, but a collaborated family of plans covering every aspect of what we jointly knew to be the most important factors clearly linked to our ends. The field offices were set and began distributing the resources as promised in a combination of both trucks and helicopters, where necessary, and both sides were enjoying an unprecedented level of cooperation and satisfaction.

The fall period had seemed mild, but the winter was fast approaching and the demand for energy was soon to peak. Our systems approach had anticipated this and we were gearing up to provide the supplies and services needed.

The first reports of long lines at the butane station didn't concern me much. I had built up a certain tolerance to the ebb and flow of front-line operational challenges. From time to time we were often faced with making do until supplies could be freed up from the provider. I do remember, though, when it struck me that this winter was not going to be as I had imagined.

The diplomatic démarches had started in early spring, but the impasses had not seemed so severe and appeared likely to resolve over time. They had not. In fact, they had widened. The main pass through the mountains had too many vulnerabilities. Our host nation's military commander could not cover them all. The U.S. Congress had been lulled to sleep regarding sending more resources in the form of security personnel and U.S. aid because everything had been going so well with the plan. It was too late.

The neighboring country shut down the pass to the east. The trickle of supplies from elsewhere began to threaten our objectives of stability as so many locals had come to rely on this outside help until they could provide for themselves in the countryside. The rebels took first dibs, and the dwindling supplies to the local people caused a furor. Village militia formed to grab what little was left from the relief trucks as they fanned out to address the concerned areas. Security was weak because there had been no resources committed to this contingency.

I was distraught but determined not to lose my head, or my job, over this situation. Our systems thinking had gotten us this far and we had properly identified the right aiming points, or ends, for our plans, and I wasn't about to let a little thing like supplies get in the way of our goals. The local people would just have to show a little backbone. They had had a hard life before we arrived in their country, couldn't they just call upon their resilience to get through a few additional months without heat and light in their homes?

The Econistan press called the flap an example of all that is wrong with U.S. foreign policy – a policy of creating dependence and ultimately hegemony over a disparate people. The U.S. President was unable to sustain support from the American people as they rose in unity to declare that America's image in the world could not afford another decade of such bad publicity. We had crawled out of a hole once before, and we were not about to crawl back into it. The scheduled donors' conference had also been canceled in protest at the U.S. position, as perceived in many international capitals. This policy had to end.

My staff said their goodbyes to the local hires we had come to know and love. The host military was attempting a surge of security in the pass region, but the real progress would come upon our leaving. Once the last U.S. transport's wheels lifted off the ground in Econistan, the neighboring country released its blockade of the pass and the crisis passed. The winter sealed in the rebels, who were subdued by the relief in supplies. But without our presence, I watched on TV that next summer as the President of Econistan was ousted and there was talk of a U.S. military intervention. I couldn't watch anymore.

<u>The Main Lesson:</u> Without an integrated set of means aimed toward supporting the ways for accomplishing an end, there can be no effective end accomplishment.

In our story, I had learned the following:

- I had understood only the very basics of the necessity of means or resources. My systems thinking had identified this issue area but I had not truly matched my means to my ways and ends, especially for situations that might be unexpected. I had learned the absolutely critical lesson of how resources could undo even the best laid plans, and I heard the echo of my early military education repeating how amateurs talk strategy while professionals talk logistics.

- I had learned to open my aperture in my systems thinking to include a robust early and constant assessment and reassessment of the potential resources obstacles, and I pledged never again to let this become my Achilles' heel.

- The ways of getting the supplies were also linked to the means problem. Because of early decisions to go heavy on ground traffic rather than air, as carried over from the previous dream, there were few options left to alleviate the situation.

PART V: KEY FUNCTIONS SUPPORTING THE PARADIGM

Now the real nuts and bolts. With the preceding nine-part paradigm in place, the functions of my proposed planning and execution management system includes the following, with a description of each below:

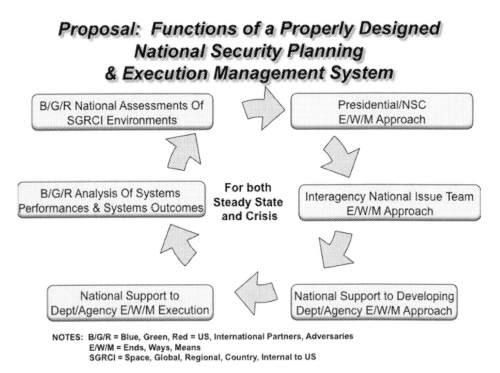

Figure 2

These are the Functions that Would be Performed in the NAVIC

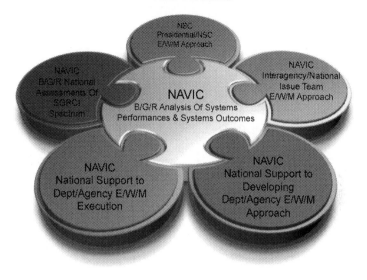

Figure 3

1. National Assessments run by a Director for National Assessments for both geographical and functional threats and opportunities spanning the concentric and inclusive spectrums of Space, the Globe, Specific Regions and/or Sub-Regions, Specific Countries within Regions, and the United States internally (the 'SGRCI' spectrums) in the near-, mid- and long- term across the adversarial sectors (Red), other partner sectors (Green) and the U.S. sectors (Blue).

- National Assessments will include Living Intelligence Community Assessment Reports on Threats and Opportunities (Red) across the spectrums of SGRCI as authorized at Strategic, Operational and Tactical levels for the near, mid and long term.

- Additionally, National Assessments will include Living Whole-of-Government Interagency, Private Sector and International Actor (Blue/Green) Assessment Reports (outside intelligence community) on Threats and Opportunities across SGRCI matters at Strategic, Operational and Tactical levels for the near, mid and long term.

- Finally, theses will be collated by the NAVIC professionals and presented not as one report but separately in the context of appropriate environmental Strategic Risks.

(NOTE: 'Living' implies that all necessary baseline information and capabilities are 'alive' in that they are not static but rather dynamic and ever-evolving. In a practical sense, to be living, baseline information on U.S. and multinational public and private sector roles, missions and capabilities must already reside on a master database or in reality from which to quickly assess, dynamically rearrange and reconnect to reassert new directions at a moment's notice.)

These National Assessments flow to the next step in the chain of the planning and execution management system – National Policy Formulation.

2. <u>National Policy Formulation.</u> (NOTE for the far-off future but not for this proposal in the near term: I personally don't believe that we should use words such as 'policy,' 'strategy' or 'plans.' They are too confusing.

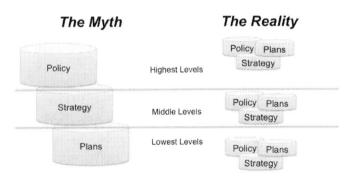

Today's Policy/Strategies/Plans

Figure 4

I would rather replace them all with the word 'approaches' to various ends, ways and means problem sets at different levels from the president to the Presidential Issue Team to the Department and so forth out to the field. These approaches would each contain the necessary integration of the ends, ways and means at those particular levels. We would then all get away from the confusing and sometimes stultifying cultural norms that often prevent folks at all levels from really believing they are allowed to think about such things as ends, ways and means at all levels. Today, no one would consider allowing a U.S. Provincial Reconstruction Team director to make 'policy' because policy is only synonymous with national level thinking. We can't afford this anymore. Field events can and often do have national implications. Policy is, after all, essentially a statement about ends – the aims of a mission or program – nothing more. Strategy and Plans are the ways and means of that mission or program. Cleary a Provincial Reconstruction Team director does design ends for his province every day.

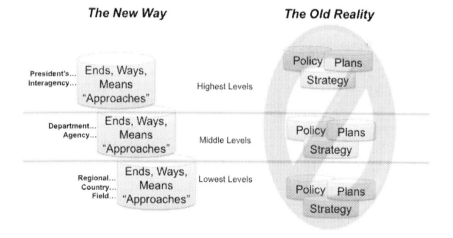

"Approaches" vs. "Policy/Strategies/Plans"

Figure 5

This may be a bridge too far to suggest the replacement of our confused traditional lexicon, but I wanted to get you thinking. Now back to using words you all recognize.)

National Policy Formulation run by a Director for National Policy Formulation starting with an articulation of the president's 50-, 25- and 10-year National Security Visions (detailed descriptions of all the parts of the national security system working together as a whole successfully in different future contexts). In addition to these Visions, the president also articulates his/her overarching intent that includes clear descriptions of end state conditions for success with overarching purposes for these ends along with broad outlines of basic ways and the broad scope of means willing (at what risk) to commit across SGRCI in the near, mid and long term in consultation with the actors at the operational and tactical levels.

(NOTE: The term 'operational' here is not specifically associated with an organizational or geographical *level* but rather the mental and physical support between strategic and tactical, where the former meets the latter, and bridges are created so that both interact without countering the other. This term originally came from the military as a result of the greater separation in time and space in the 20th century between the strategic and tactical levels of military operations because of greater weapons and transportation ranges, intelligence gathering and advanced communications technologies. The operational was born to bridge these two levels as they got more dispersed and complex. As an easy example, the president certainly can't give orders to a direct line supervisor in the field, he needs a translation mechanism. Conversely, that direct line supervisor in the field needs help understanding and, often, physically accomplishing his/her tasks, and the president can't help from his/her far-off strategic perch. These examples are extreme, but the point is made that both need an intermediary.)

- Policy Formulation starts with the president's 50-, 25- and 10-year Visions for the National Security System (a detailed description of all the parts of the national security system working together as a whole successfully in different future contexts), developed by the president, his Cabinet and NSC staff, and coordinated by the Director of National Security in sessions facilitated by permanent visioning professionals in the NAVIC. Each Vision provides context to the succeeding Vision, all the way to the president's budget forecasts. Notwithstanding the political nature of changing administrations and their corresponding mandates from the people, this process should endeavor to find some semblance of lasting effect through the transparent nature of the Vision published for all the people of the United States to read and understand. After all, the realization of such a national vision will require the people's consent and participation. In effect, national elections should become in part a referendum on these Visions. The Director for National Security and the NSC staff will create this document with assistance from professional, full-time facilitators, bringing in outside experts from the appropriate fields of expertise in both the public and private sectors as necessary to accomplish this task. These visioning sessions will be conducted in the newly constructed National Assessment, Visioning and Integration Center (NAVIC) located on the National Mall (a proposal to be discussed later in greater detail).

- As noted earlier, and in the contexts set by the National Visions, National Policy will be in part articulated though a Living National Security Planning Guidance for National Security Missions and Programs articulating only the president's overarching Intent [clear descriptions of end state conditions for success with overarching purposes for key ends, broad outlines of basic ways, and the broad scope of means willing (at what risk) to commit] in the near, mid and long term for each of the SGRCI spectrums at the strategic level but in consultation with the actors at the operational and tactical levels, and including any additional Mission Specific Guidance Statements to particular lead department, agency, Presidential Issue Teams or state governor as needed. (The idea of a National Security Planning Guidance is not a new idea and most recently derived from the PNSR in their report, "Forging a New Shield." The idea that it be living and the description of what it contains is original here.)

This unprecedented consultation process should also be formalized equally with executive and legislative advisory and oversight organizations to promote early and high, transparent and parallel support. Without this, there can be no nimble or dynamic reassertion of direction as situations change and evolve. The imperative of core and surge will be undone without this close and dynamic unprecedented cooperation. This document would be created and distributed to all those participating in both a classified and unclassified form by the Director of National Security through the NSC with assistance from the professional facilitators and outside experts from the appropriate fields of expertise in both the public and private sectors as necessary, all facilitated at the Executive Office of the president's National Assessment, Visioning and Integration Center.

- The NAVIC would house the Red Teaming/Scenario-based Policy gaming capabilities and provide analysis from trained professionals on the outcomes of various key policy considerations played against likely contingencies.

- Presidential Resource Requests (Annual Budget Request, Six-Year Budget Request, along with 10-, 25- and 50-year Budget Estimates, all contained in the National Security Resource Document) orchestrated by the Director of National Security with the Office of Management and Budget (OMB) six months after the latest Living National Security Planning Guidance is issued to allow consultation with informed participating national security departments, agencies, Presidential Issue Teams, state governments, General Accounting Office, the OMB, and proposed Select Committee for Interagency Affairs in the Congress. (The idea of a six-year budget is also a recommendation of the PNSR.)

This unprecedented involvement of Congressional oversight offices early and high in the executive process, along with the increased long-term budget estimates coinciding with the president's Vision and after the issuance of the National Security Planning Guidance, will force transparency and long-term contextual thinking in both branches of government while mitigating competition and building trust.

- As always, the NAVIC will provide assessments of Strategic Risks and Trade-offs of these National Policy Formulation documents.

These National Policy Formulation documents flow to the next step in the chain of the planning and execution management system – National Strategy Making.

3. <u>National Strategy Making</u> run by the Director for National Strategy Making for the articulation of the specific how and who of the national integration of national Ends, Ways and Means (including Congressional support) in support of overarching Presidential Vision and Intent (articulated through the national policy guidance) across the SGRCI at the strategic level but in consultation with the actors at the operational and tactical levels for the near, mid and long term.
- National Strategy Making will chiefly include the creation and distribution of a Living National Security Grand Strategy to replace the defunct National Security Strategy process of previous administrations. The new National Security Grand Strategy is based on the new National Security Planning Guidance issued in the previous step, which describes the president's broad Intent for the overall integration of the national Ends, Ways and Means. The Grand Strategy turns the president's ideas into actual tasks and/or mission and program assignments for specific national security actors across SGRCI spectrums at the strategic level but informed by operational and tactical levels as appropriate for the near, mid and long term. The National Security Grand Strategy process is facilitated by permanent professionals from the Executive Office of the President, chiefly housed in the NAVIC, and is distributed at both the classified and unclassified levels and is guided by the framework illustrated in the upcoming dream sequence.
- As before in the policy formulation step, the strategy-making step will benefit from Red Teaming/Scenario-based game analysis on all aspects of the Grand Strategy, facilitated by the strategy development professionals within the NAVIC.

- The Strategy-making step will include the president's issue of a national security budget that includes both an annual request and a six-year estimate orchestrated by the Director of National Security, including the various national security actors and oversight organizations, in coordination with the OMB and, finally, approved by the president.

- The Grand Strategy will include a National Security Strategic Human Capital Plan (also recommended by the PNSR's 2008 "Forging a New Shield") approved by the DNS but orchestrated by the Office of Personnel Management.

- The Grand Strategy will include a National Security Knowledge Management Plan approved by the DNS but orchestrated by a new National Knowledge Management Office located in the Executive Office of the President.

- Again, the NAVIC will provide assessments of Strategic Risks and Trade-offs within the National Grand Strategy and accompanying documents.

These National Grand Strategy documents flow to the next step in the chain of the planning and execution management system – National Planning Support.

4. <u>National Planning Support</u> run by the Director for National Planning Support located in the NAVIC to support subordinate state, U.S. department, agency and/or Presidential Issue Teams in the creation of their own strategic, operational and tactical plans for the near, mid and long term across the SGRCI spectrums that articulate a clear integration of their use of their portion of the national Ends, Ways and Means.

- The NAVIC will provide reach-back Red-Teaming/Scenario-based gaming support and analysis from its professionals to these state, U.S. department, agency and Mission Teams as requested.

- The NAVIC will provide assistance teams when possible to conduct short-term, onsite, independent observation and coaching for these subordinate teams in mission planning as well as support to facilitated mission rehearsals. The NAVIC will also offer its facilities for facilitated rehearsals, as space is available.

These national planning support efforts flow to the next step in the chain of the planning and execution management system – National Implementation Support.

5. National Implementation Support run by the Director for National Implementation Support to support the subordinate actions and actors implementing their portion of the national Ends, Ways and Means across the organizations operating in the different SGRCI spectrums at the strategic, operational and tactical levels for the near, mid and long term.

- At the direction of the DNS, the NAVIC provides fully integrated support (from the Executive Office of the President) to state, U.S. department, agency and/or Presidential Issue Teams to subordinate implementation teams as available, managing reach-back answers from the Executive Office of the President on Requests for Information.

- The NAVIC assists the DNS and the NSC in issuing and tracking Policy Adjudication Change Papers where national level contradictions and conflicts arise affecting subordinate actors.

- The NAVIC orchestrates full reach-back support to Red-Teaming/ Scenario-based gaming and analysis in support of the actions to integrate the subordinates' portions of the national Ends, Ways and Means across the organizations operating in the different SGRCI spectrums at the strategic, operational and tactical levels.

- The NAVIC provides onsite planning and execution management assistance teams to subordinates when possible to conduct short-term independent observation and coaching in mission execution management, as well as support to facilitated mission rehearsals. The NAVIC will offer facilities for facilitated rehearsals, as space is available.

- Provide connectivity of operational and tactical implementation budget obligations, requests for funds transfer, additional budget forecasts to the national strategic budget processes, based on tracking of implementation progress according to agreed-upon measureable metrics tied to key objectives and goals. Offer metrics professionals to assist as required.

6. National Operational Analysis run by the Director for National Operational Analysis of all the elements of the internal systems' planning and execution management processes across the spectrums of SGRCI expressed through lessons learned, with agreed-upon metrics to identify necessary internal system improvements in the near, mid and long term.

   - A 'Living' National Security Review (capturing baselines of operational roles, missions and capabilities of U.S. national security system actors) conducted by offices of the NAVIC. This one element of the planning and execution management system combined with the Living Assessments are chiefly responsible for enabling the 'living' National Security Planning Guidance and the subsequent National Security Grand Strategy. This living process enables unprecedented smooth transitions from steady state to contingency responses and back to steady state across the entirety of the U.S. government.

   - At the direction of the DNS, the NAVIC will also orchestrate an Annual Lessons Learned report on National Security Planning and Execution Management across SGRCI at Strategic, Operational and Tactical levels of missions and systems using appropriate metrics.

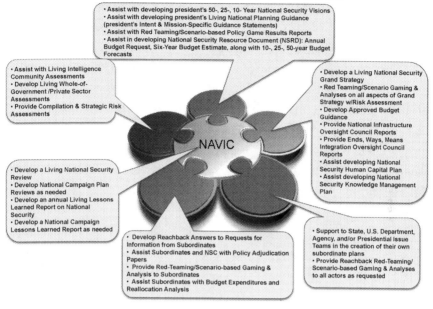

NAVIC Process/Products

- Assist with developing president's 50-, 25-, 10- Year National Security Visions
- Assist with developing president's Living National Planning Guidance (president's Intent & Mission-Specific Guidance Statements)
- Assist with Red Teaming/Scenario-based Policy Game Results Reports
- Assist in developing National Security Resource Document (NSRD): Annual Budget Request, Six-Year Budget Estimate, along with 10-, 25-, 50-year Budget Forecasts

- Assist with Living Intelligence Community Assessments
- Develop Living Whole-of-Government /Private Sector Assessments
- Provide Compilation & Strategic Risk Assessments

- Develop a Living National Security Grand Strategy
- Red Teaming/Scenario Gaming & Analyses on all aspects of Grand Strategy w/Risk Assessment
- Develop Approved Budget Guidance
- Provide National Infrastructure Oversight Council Reports
- Provide Ends, Ways, Means Integration Oversight Council Reports
- Assist developing National Security Human Capital Plan
- Assist developing National Security Knowledge Management Plan

- Develop a Living National Security Review
- Develop National Campaign Plan Reviews as needed
- Develop an annual Living Lessons Learned Report on National Security
- Develop a National Campaign Lessons Learned Report as needed

- Develop Reachback Answers to Requests for Information from Subordinates
- Assist Subordinates and NSC with Policy Adjudication Papers
- Provide Red-Teaming/Scenario-based Gaming & Analysis to Subordinates
- Assist Subordinates with Budget Expenditures and Reallocation Analysis

- Support to State, U.S. Department, Agency, and/or Presidential Issue Teams in the creation of their own subordinate plans
- Provide Reachback Red-Teaming/Scenario-based Gaming & Analyses to all actors as requested

NAVIC

Figure 6

Before any of this can become a reality, these products and processes must be gamed in stages through a piloting program over a period of years to identify how the theoretical can move to the practical and how the sum total of products and processes will equal a complete and understandable holistic narrative for the presidential management of the integration of the national Ends, Ways and Means in the planning and execution of national security.

The six functional directors (whose appointments should be Senate confirmed for fifteen-year tenures and whose positions would reside within the NAVIC) would not supplant any part of the president's relationships to and with his/her Cabinet or NSC staff. Rather, they would focus on providing 'push' services to the existing formal and informal systems of decision-making.

Finally, the new Director of National Security (DNS) would be responsible for the management of all six of the functions of a National Security Planning and Execution Management System but would have a deputy to act as Executive Director for the NAVIC. The DNS may spend the majority of his/her time in the Policy Formulation phase with an emphasis on all the various aspects of garnering Congressional support for resources and appropriate oversight as well as early and high process participation from the whole of government and multilateral/multinational actors. The Deputy DNS ensures overall coordination of the NAVIC services to those policies and the president's staff and Cabinet secretaries. Each of the functional directors would work directly for the Deputy DNS.

Dream Sequence 5 (Planning and Execution are Part of the Same Whole):

The first six months had finally come and gone and we were preparing for the donors' conference after the winter thaw had reached its zenith. The fuel crisis, which had threatened to bring everything to a halt, had been alleviated by strong strategic regional diplomacy coupled to local action by key leaders to keep the supplies crossing through the passes.

I had not heard from the President of Econistan in nearly a month – a sign that tensions were low. He was abroad at the moment and we would meet in the capital of the European lead nation for the international donors' conference. There we would make our pitch to garner the necessary means to support the way we were achieving our ends. The plans were carefully laid and confidence was riding reasonably high.

On a hunch, and knowing that situations can change at a moment's notice, and having suffered the consequences of my previous inflexibility, I wanted to spend a moment with my staff to make sure there wouldn't be any surprises while I was away in Europe. I would be gone for approximately ten days, so both the nation's top leaders and I would be out of the country at the same time.

I gathered my planning staff and noticed the comments I had given to them earlier were reflected in their slide presentations back to me. It seemed as if my planning staff was on the right path and understood my guidance and my vision. They were real pros. I felt lucky to have their creative influences on the future of our work. Now all it would take is for the execution team to implement their great work – no questions asked.

The messenger whispered in my ear right in the middle of the President of Econistan's address to the assembled European body. As I opened the note he passed me, I could tell that my departure from the meeting hall would be permanent. I was headed on the next transport out.

Insurgents had captured and killed ninety-seven people in three separate attacks in the north at three separate weddings. The president's second–in-charge had been captured and was missing. His daughter, one of the brides, was among the dead.

The President of Econistan joined me that night and our collective planning staffs gathered to review possible ways ahead. As the briefings ensued, my sometimes-irritating operations director asked if he could be a part of the planning session along with several members of his staff. When I refused, he announced that had it not been for a similar dismissal of his operations (or execution) staff from the last planning meeting before I had left for Europe, they might have exposed the insurgents' intentions before they had gotten out of hand.

Embarrassed and suspicious, I nevertheless acquiesced and asked him to present his assertions. To my astonishment that night, I learned of a troubling process flaw endemic to my headquarters that had systematically prevented the right sharing of ground operational truth with future planning. The plans that I was making with my team of so-called pros were devised completely in a vacuum from the realities transpiring on the front lines. We had been basing our plans on a false sense of security. The situation had, in fact, been teetering on the brink even before I left Econistan and, had I known, the recent calamities could have been averted. The donors' conference ended abruptly, indefinitely postponed as a result of these developments.

The situation was eventually rectified as I formed new teaming processes to encourage the full breadth of both planning and execution to be performed as one symbiotic process. From then on, each group exchanged liaisons and both shops presented to me together in the same room.

The donors' conference eventually reconvened and the process for creating stability in Econistan survived for another day.

<u>The Main Lesson:</u> Across the ends, ways and means continuum, both planning and execution must be intertwined as equals where planners and execution managers have a balance between being sequestered

alone to do what they are best at and being thrown together from time to time to share and reach equilibrium on information and each others' perspectives.

<u>In our story, I had learned the following:</u>

- Ends, Ways and Means systems integration has to be treated equally in both the planning and execution as one leading into the other and back again.

- Plans have to be based on ground truth as much as possible or they aren't worth a dime.

- Execution personnel have to provide ground truth to planners, including, perhaps most especially, resource or means planners. Trade-offs and forecasts for donors' conferences, the U.S. Congress, or for any other capital or host nation cannot occur unless ground truth is the basis. This becomes especially challenging as the situation evolves.

- No system of thinking and doing can be complete if these two parts are treated as separate and distinct. They have to be treated as two sides of a single coin, and National Team Leaders must set the example by speaking of them often and in nearly the same breath.

PART VI: THE NATIONAL ASSESSMENT, VISIONING AND INTEGRATION CENTER (NAVIC)

There is no desire to create additional offices or bureaucratic processes within government just for the sake of it. This proposal does, however, suggest a new overall home for this massive facilitation and orchestration requirement.

The NAVIC process can be succinctly described as supporting the National Security Planning and Execution Management System in applying its six functions for the benefit of the president and all supporting actors in both the planning and execution of national security. The Center provides the president with an ability to immediately take stock of the status of both the internal system and the external environment, as well as to understand the decision points necessary to maintain his many policy objectives in the near, mid and long term across the whole of the national security system in the five SGRCI spectrums of the National Security Planning and Execution Management System.

The NAVIC offers both continuity and world-class expertise in the orchestration of, but not in decision-making or in creation of, policy or political direction. That is left strictly in the domain of the political leaders. The NAVIC is essentially a creature for the state and is made up nearly in whole by career civil servants with no political affiliations or allegiances. The NAVIC, then, becomes an essential and unprecedented tool for each president to maintain his/her own situational awareness and bring coherency to the rest of the executive branch in both planning and execution of his/her policy ends.

Moreover, if the president uses this hub to center his network of national security processes and people in the integration of the nation's ends, ways and means for national security, then it is even clearer that both the National Security Planning and Execution Management System and its NAVIC should occupy a central and prominent physical position in the U.S. government and in Washington, D.C.

- Provides services to Cabinet, NSC, Congress, Governors - does not make policy
- State-of-the-art facilities & processes
- Provide continuity in national security with expert civil servants
- Informational connectivity across breadth of actors
- Provides President multiple redundant command center capabilities
- Emphasis on Visual aspects of understanding
- Emphasis on long-term thinking and doing
- Managed by one politically appointed director who works for the DNS
- Run by six 15-year appointed assistant directors for each function

Figure 7

The Center would employ state-of-the-art facilities and decision support tools operating in both classified and unclassified collaborative domains. Its data would be shared virtually and its processes replicated in similar sites around the country. In fact, any appropriate site in the world will be able to replicate this capability, offering near-perfect resiliency, scale and uninterrupted service to the president during any national or global emergency.

As such, its processes and data would be shared and replicated in the White House Situation Room as well as onboard Air Force One, at Camp David, etc., in a real-time persistent manner. The NAVIC would be the model for complete refurbishment of the present Situation Room in order to accomplish this (the author acknowledges the recent post 9-11 improvements of the Situation Room/s but suggests much more can be done). All of the president's key deliberation offices would share the exact same collaborative information backbone as well as advanced visual knowledge sharing systems for command and control and advanced networked analysis. Moreover, each of the departments and agencies, as well as all state governors, will replicate similar capabilities in their domains.

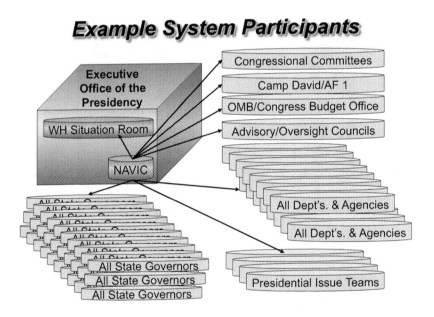

Figure 8

At any time, any of these satellite 'mini NAVICs' could become the president's command and control center if needed in a national emergency. As Presidential Issue Teams are formed, the National

Knowledge Management Office in the NAVIC will be ready with exportable knowledge management packages of both hardware and software to bring these teams online within twenty-four hours. Congress would also have its own mini-NAVIC connectivity to achieve the unprecedented new collaboration called for in the National Security Planning and Execution Management System. Finally, all subordinate elements of the National Security Planning and Execution Management System, from the Strategic to the Tactical, would enjoy connectivity so that bottom-up ground truth would only be a click away.

As stated earlier, the NAVIC Executive Director would be a Senate-confirmed member of the Executive Office of the President, working also as the Deputy Director of National Security. With the exception of the politically appointed Assistant Directors and the two executive/legislative oversight councils, the majority of the rest of the staff would be full-time civil servants, to provide continuity between administrations.

The NAVIC will consider the president and his NSC staff as its primary customers. At all times the NAVIC should be seen as following, not leading, the president and his staff of policy designers, and would endeavor to be value-added in both timeliness and substance to the particular decision-making processes put in place by the president. The NAVIC's secondary but equally important customers will be the remaining executive and legislative actors in the national security community, as designated.

The staff size would be significant given the functions required. Consider a single Combatant Commander staff of hundreds just to keep up with the integration of the ends, ways and means of a single regional military policy. The six broad National Security Planning and Execution Management System functions with the proposed product outputs will determine the final form, but one can imagine the immense workload.

A very rough order of magnitude is that 225 to 250 permanent personnel will be required. Some organizational experts will suggest this figure must be much higher but this needs not be so and must not be so to maintain effectiveness. What it can't get done, it simply won't, and that will mean setting better priorities. It must not become, however, a bloated bureaucracy in only a few years time. This core must remain lean for decades to come. Advisors and contractors from outside government would likely be a part of this workforce and may represent as much as twenty percent of its hires, primarily as part-timers in order to keep the Center nimble and on the cutting edge of evolving technologies, education, and processes for its mission accomplishment.

New structures will need to be created to allow for the individual office spaces, but also for numerous medium-to-large collaborative working spaces and briefing rooms, each with all the necessary visual brainstorming equipment ergonomically designed to elicit the best thinking (there will be many existing and future designs to review).

As a reminder, the Center would essentially be designed around the six functions and the following corresponding functional directors:

The Director for National Assessments would coordinate the national level geographical and functional threats and opportunities assessments and risk analysis spanning the inclusive SGRCI spectrums of space, the globe, specific regions and/or sub-regions, specific countries within regions, and the United States internally in the near, mid and long term.

The Director for National Policy Formulation would help game and facilitate the articulation of the president's 50-, 25- and 10-year National Security Visions (detailed descriptions of all the parts of the national security system working together as a whole successfully in different future contexts). In addition to these Visions, the Center will assist the president in articulating his overarching intent [clear descriptions of end-state conditions for success with overarching purposes for key ends, broad outlines of basic ways, and the broad scope of means willing (at what risk) to commit] across SGRCI in the near, mid, and long term for the strategic level, but in consultation with the actors at the operational and tactical levels.

The Director for National Strategy Making would direct the articulation of the specific 'how' and 'who' of the national integration of ways and means (including Congressional support) in support of overarching presidential ends articulated through his Vision and Intent (Policy Guidance) across the SGRCI at the strategic level, but in consultation with the actors at the operational and tactical levels for the near, mid and long term.

The Director for National Planning Support would coordinate the national support to state, U.S. department, agency, and/or Presidential Issue Teams in the creation of their own strategic, operational and tactical plans for the immediate to near, mid and long term across SGRCI that articulate a clear integration of their ends, ways and means.

The Director for National Implementation Support would coordinate national support to the subordinate actors implementing their ways with the appropriate means across the organizations operating in the different SGRCI spectrums at the operational and tactical levels in the near, mid and long term.

The Director for National Operational Analysis would coordinate a lessons-learned regime within the National Security Planning and Execution Management System using agreed-upon metrics to identify necessary internal system improvements in the near, mid and long term aimed at improving system outcomes.

Each Director would have a deputy and staff of approximately thirty personnel. Each of these would be a validated member of the new National Security Professional Corps. Each of these five-year Senate-confirmed Directors should be at a Senior Executive Service rank commensurate with the level needed to garner the support required to achieve their specific functions across the breadth of the national security establishment (and perhaps also with private sector and international partners).

Dream Sequence 6 (Near, Mid, Long):

I finally had my first restful sleep in nearly a month. The experience I was gaining was beginning to hit real pay dirt. I had avoided a donors' conference catastrophe and the President of Econistan, although initially stunned by the wedding massacres, had made the necessary adjustments to his own staffs such that both planners and operators were working together as one.

The next spring and summer passed and we were all on our second year without a mission-ending set of events. Our systems approach had integrated the ends, ways and means in both planning and execution. Our staff was beginning to start its first rotation homeward and I had to say goodbye to many a good friend and colleague.

Elections were coming soon as well, and it was no foregone conclusion that the President of Econistan would succeed in remaining in power. My new staff had begun the process of working with experts and the local administration on preparing to ensure that the safety and fairness of the elections were a priority. There had been too much progress made to let electoral problems undermine the legitimacy of our collective efforts with the people and the rebel leaders.

That night, I entertained some of the new international staff members from various development and diplomatic circles at a dinner in a nearby restaurant. I was struck by the tone of the conversation given the recent progress we had all made toward stability. The mood seemed to be one of less, not more, confidence in our trajectory, and I was puzzled.

There formed two camps on this matter. In one camp were the concerns of the development community, who spoke in terms of decades for progress and were of the mind that nothing we had done to date had any strategic vision and so would have no lasting effect on the situation at hand. In the other camp, I found diplomats, sprinkled with a few military minded folks, who seemed to believe that we could no longer pursue our present course due to the fact that other areas of the world needed our attention more.

I left decidedly angst-ridden over what I had heard. That there could be dissenting opinion was of no matter, but that I was persuaded equally by both arguments was very disconcerting. I drifted off to sleep with this on my mind.

My discomfort came at a most inauspicious moment, as I was about to leave for the States for my first visit home to see both the president and my family in nearly eighteen months. My trip's purpose would be to recommend to the president, based on a complete systems assessment, what U.S. policy and strategy ought to be in the near future, as his election was also coinciding with that of the President of Econistan. Here I would be in a dilemma. I was slowly coming to realize that the diplomatic/military community was winning out in their campaign to make the case to the U.S. president for a full withdrawal from Econistan. On the other hand, the development community coupled to the local situation, including the President of Econistan's plea and his reelection concerns, had increasingly persuaded me toward a direction away from my own president. A withdrawal did not seem reasonable, but since I did not have a long-term analysis completed by my staff, I was prepared only with my intuition spurred by the one dinner conversation. This would surely not be enough to persuade the president.

I felt defenseless as I walked into the White House Situation Room that April morning. My staff had been focused on the immediate for most of my eighteen-month tenure. Expediency in crisis had taught me to pay most attention to the actions closest in front of me. Now, both a U.S. and Econistan election were on the horizon and my budding strategy seemed doomed to help one over the other in what increasingly seemed like an either/or proposition. Was this an either/or proposition? Was there no middle ground? I would never know because I had not created a staff capable of, nor had I set the proper example of, considering and weighing multiple options for the near-, mid- and long-term consequences of our actions on the overall end accomplishment.

As the president smiled after my staff presentation, he asked if I had anything else to add. I could not bring myself to answer to my convictions. The political pressure was too much and my lack of alternative option development addressing the true impact of the president's policy to withdraw had been my fault. I would have to live with that for the rest of my life.

Many years later, I served on a panel at a local think tank conference. The U.S. administration had changed by then. The previous president had won his initial reelection, but his party was swept out of power in the following election when his withdrawal from Econistan resulted in an overthrow of that government. In my mind this overthrow had been a rejection of three years of hard work. I could only hang my head a bit as the questions from the audience pelted my sense of what could have been.

Had I been able to plan with both the long term as well as the near term in mind, I might have been able to present the U.S. president with another option to consider – one that was not an either/or choice. As time had worn on, I grew to care less in the end about the U.S. politics at stake. In my own long run, I found myself caring more about the fate of all those I failed to represent in that wonderful country so far away. I had succumbed to my own local politics and the momentum of the immediate.

I left the conference and, as I was driving home, resolved to write all my experiences down in the hope of helping the next guy or gal get it right in spite of such pressures. I would help teach the next team how to think in the long term as well as in the immediate. The next day, I sat at my computer and began to type ....

The Main Lesson: Ends, ways and means integration across both planning and execution is not enough if ill-considered across the appropriate time contexts. Without some outer context to each inner concentric circle of time dimension, there can be no balanced or wise application of any of the ends, ways and means. As these concentric time circles are considered 'out' from the immediate problem or opportunity focal point, it is natural for the utility of such considerations to fade. That said, it should not be an excuse for not trying. The proverbial butterfly effect begins in these outer rings – the long-term horizons – and the goal should be to identify the flapping wings as they so harmlessly affect airflows around them before their ripple effects cause tropical storms to form across the Pacific. Seriously, context is everything and no effort should be spared to discern all contexts as thoroughly as possible.

<u>In our story, I had learned the following:</u>

- Planning and Execution Management in both the long term and the short-term is hard, but it demands a respect that only true professionals, or maybe just those with both common sense and the ability to speak truth to power, can muster.

- Just as plans and operations are two sides of a coin, so too are long- and short-term planning and execution. Sometimes one will cancel the other out. Sometimes one will lead to new insights for the other, and this is not only true in the sequential direction from the long to the short. Sometimes short-term planning can reveal longer-term needs and vice versa.

- In the main, though, I learned that longer-term thinking provides for the necessary context for shorter-term planning and execution. Without the former, the latter is at great risk, and sometimes the risks can prove to be catastrophic.

PART VII: VISUALIZING THE NAVIC IN ACTION

The NAVIC should be the venue of choice for the president to get a fix on national security. Jargon aside, at any time the president should be able to turn to the Director of the NAVIC for an objective, comprehensive picture – sometimes literally - of how the administration's national security ends, ways and means are being addressed across all SGRCI spectrums according to presidential policy priorities. The White House Situation Room and accompanying suites received improvements following the 9-11 attacks, but even these enhancements fall far short of the possibilities for a new capability to truly 'see' the system at work and its possible trajectories based on state-of-the-art visualization techniques. To help you see how this might come together, the following scenario is offered.

Imagine entering a comfortably small, lightly colored, carpeted room with earth-tone walls and tiered lighting that covers the area in a pleasant glow. The furniture is mostly modern art deco leather, moderately plush, all on wheels so that the room can take any shape depending on the moment's needs.

There are no tables except for the small, pullout tabletops on each leather armchair that can switch over to either left or right-handed use, each complete with drink holder to contain the beverage offered upon entering.

Upon sitting, and with a push of button, screens lower and lights dim for an opening ten-minute presentation by the automated prebriefing multimedia show.

The president hears the proposed agenda of the meeting he is about to chair in the next room (the NAVIC's most inner sanctum, called the 'Think Room'), along with a prescreening of the likely talking points of the members about to join him. A short discussion ensues with his closest advisors.

At the same time, in the main room, the remaining meeting participants are receiving a similar preparation in order to set the proper mood and group dynamics. Two senior NAVIC professionals assigned to play key roles in shaping the group dynamics join this group. The first role is that of 'blocker' or 'challenger' to the issues about to be discussed. He/she hails from the NAVIC's Red Team. This blocker role is performed with appropriate aplomb commensurate with presidential decision-making, but this role player, of some stature of his own, will ensure no groupthink goes unchallenged and may encourage others to expound on their own differing perspectives.

The second role player is that of the observer. He/she will be expected to observe the proceedings silently, looking for objective results through the haze of sometimes-irrational thinking. He/she is an expert on group dynamics and cognitive bias psychology, while also a valuable member of the planning staff in the NAVIC.

Both presentations end and the two groups join each other in the Think Room. Both of these rooms are located below surface level but the shape, airflow, coloration, egg-shaped ergonomics and tiered lighting, along with the multiple layers of various automated visual aids and circular head table, make for an inviting experience. The emphasis is on achieving the most efficient transfer of information from the sender to the receiver at all times.

The chairs have mesh backings and customized adjustment controls. In front of each seat at the head table is a computer screen and keyboard with an attached electronic drawing pad and pen, beside each of which lays a multimedia remote wand. Large screens occupy a prominent position on both ends of the circular table, but with a push of a button, additional screens descend behind each seat to create an even more intimate setting and allow each participant to have his/her own information shown on the personal screen. All participants at the head table (no more than twelve at a time) have corresponding screens. With a click, the room manager automatically adjusts special additional light fixtures, moveable and flexible in the ceiling, as the meeting gets underway.

Others invited, up to twenty-five in the Think Room, are positioned around the room and view the proceedings on screens fashioned on rollers attached to interior pillars, allowing for 360-degree rotation of the screens around the pillar in order to adjust to any direction for any viewing angle. These screens, and others positioned around the room, provide the same images to those on the outside of the inner circle as the images those on the inside are seeing. All screens are able to accommodate multiple presentations using split-screen technologies.

Any participant can use his or her drawing pad at any time to 'drive' a drawing on-screen at full-screen mode so that every participant can see the sketch on their own 24-inch monitors in front of them or on the lowered five-by-seven-feet screens directly across from them behind each participant. The computer monitors are all inset into the tabletops to allow eye-to-eye contact with all members and the president around the meeting table during these discussions.

Audio and video performance matches Blu-ray-like technologies so that any 'virtual' attendee is shown life-sized with near perfection from screens emanating upwards from the floor in the open center space of the circular table setup. These four-foot tall screens with accompanying surround sound, tops angled backwards to the center, each perched on a "lazy Susan" base, would rotate slowly, displaying participants from anywhere around the world. When a person on-screen speaks to the president, that rotating screen will rotate to face the president.

The drop-down screens lift, the discussions end, the data is captured and all notes and assignments are already resident in the collaborative knowledge management architecture so that every participant can either access them immediately from authorized mobile devices on the way out the door or from their parent organization PC when they arrive back at their respective bases. All this has saved time and allowed for maximum focus.

But the gathering doesn't completely end; it only shifts to the next room. The next room, however, is no longer subterranean. The president and his inner circle ascend to the top floor of the newly-built NAVIC to an admirable skyline viewed through the floor-to-ceiling windows spanning a 45-foot panoramic vista. The conversation continues unclassified and refreshments are made available. The president departs after twenty minutes and the rest continue their talks for the remaining hour.

Meanwhile, the Executive Director of the Center has moved on to her office, adjacent to the top floor social room, to tend to the next series of priorities, leaving her Deputy behind to finish the formal duties with the guests. The Executive Director decides to visit her Assistant Director for Strategy Making. On her way down in the elevator, she passes each floor, which house a different Assistant Director and his/her functional staff. At the third floor above ground, she steps off and heads towards the Assistant Director's office. The Director notes with some interest that many of the gaming rooms she passes along the way are occupied with studious professionals covering the floor-to-ceiling whiteboard walls with dry erasable ideas.

She passes through the center of these rooms, all outwardly facing with views to the noonday spring sun shining on the Mall. The interior office setting is filled with open egg-shaped team areas that house workstations comprised of various composite members of the national security community. The Director recalls that at the last staff meeting, the workforce expressed their satisfaction with the open workspace environment, given the augmentation of the multiple available gaming rooms, complete with remote phone and computer setups, that any user can retreat to as needed for more private work and conversations on a temporary basis. The workforce further commented how the upper deck coffee house also allows for both an escape and an additional work venue of a different kind, enormously important to a creative thinking environment.

After her visit with the Assistant Director for Strategy Making, the Director decides to get a bite to eat down on the ground floor before her panel discussion in Auditorium Number 4 with the World Futurists Society, whose D.C. office is now located on the main floor just above the lobby. This floor also houses the World Futurists Society Museum and Foundation, the former being open to the public. The Foundation, in conjunction with the president's initiative on Future Innovations for National Security across the new, broader scope of national security, from Education to Global Warming, honors annually the person or persons who have contributed the most to the future of U.S. and world security with the president's World Futurist Medal of Honor. Today, the Director will be discussing this upcoming event for the 2010 awardees.

As the day comes to a close, the Executive Director notices out of her left window, as she drives away on the George Washington Memorial Parkway, that the NAVIC stands out as a modern, colorful reminder on the D.C. skyline that this nation has finally found a way to take a small but important step toward transparency and community organizing at the U.S. government level that is breeding a new trust and confidence across the aisles. The Director feels in her gut that the 21st century has finally started to slip from its past toward real change. But there is still much work to be done.

This short scenario provides a mental image of the kinds of structural and organizational dimensions that a NAVIC could bring to enhance the virtual connectivity described in the knowledge management architecture. It also serves as a useful introduction and transition to a brief outline of some of the unique processes the NAVIC will utilize in order to provide the best service possible to its customers.

The 'visioning' component of the NAVIC is a unique and unprecedented contribution to national security. Visioning is an aspirational form of scenario use. In fact, the most useful way to introduce the use of scenarios in general is to note that scenarios are utilized by the NAVIC in one of two primary ways: 1) to stress test both policy and strategic plans' courses of action; and 2) to assist the president and any other national security organization in developing Visions for their organizations.

In the first case (stress test scenarios), trained professionals would invent scenarios that replicate the most likely environment for a potential course of action or policy objective. This process can be lengthy, but there are also a number of varying degrees of sophistication for any scenario's design and use. The NAVIC will likely focus more on the less sophisticated in terms of both length and number of role players during a tabletop exercise or more comprehensive Red Team-supported game.

The NAVIC would more often trade sophistication for timeliness, but even the simplest games orchestrated by the permanent NAVIC professionals would be infinitely more revealing than anything yet available within the interagency space of today's system. These scenarios and their tabletop exercises might last half a day or more, if necessary, and would be focused to elicit very specific insights to key aspects of any policy or plan. There are a number of variations on this concept but the intention here is only to illustrate that scenario use in this fashion would be available and ongoing daily on several fronts for multiple plans and customers at any time in the NAVIC facility.

In the second case (aspirational scenarios), trained professionals would employ specialized workshop techniques with key participants on developing Visions using multiple, plausible visualizations of futures. These futures may take the form of scenarios created in some future time, complete with sub-storylines that depict the use of, or encounter with, likely and desired aspects of a future system working together successfully as a whole.

The emphasis on the use of scenarios in this manner is to help organizational leaders 'play out' future ideas on their particular system and see what it might evolve into and how it might interact with itself and others in a future environment under different variations of that future environment. The purpose of this is to exercise and stretch the collective minds of organizations and their leaders to see the realm of the possible. From the created Visions, organizations and their leaders can return to their home bases and work on creating strategic movement toward that aspirational view of themselves in that future.

This becomes the beginning of grand strategic thinking. It is important to understand that, unlike stress test scenario use, the storylines in these scenarios are meant only to bring about a positive visualization – something to aim for.

The NAVIC, as a centerpiece to the overall presidential strategic management system, will have multiple roles and relationships to maintain. These roles and relationships will differ from one organization to the next, primarily based on the particular function it is working on. For example, in the subordinate planning and implementation stages, the NAVIC essentially offers a friendly hand and takes its cues from those planning organizations and their needs.

To each it will offer its scenario use support as well as its professional Red Teaming capabilities along with its mission rehearsal skills and its facilities. As with all things, resources are limited and choices will have to be made as to which organizations and missions receive priority support. In every case, the professionals from the NAVIC, including the Assistant Directors, will only offer support and not usurp the authorized chain of command dictated by the president to his administration. The NAVIC Directors exercise the appropriate authorities only as directed. This unprecedented form and function will be transformational in the way that the overall National Security Planning and Execution Management System performs for the nation and its leaders.

Figure 9

Dream Sequence 7 (Global Geographical and Functional Contexts):

My personal story had ended, but my protégé was about to get her first attempt at taking the helm. Kristina and her deputy, Thomas, had become quite the team, and they were more than ready. The new president was a big fan of their work. She would take on the new role as Presidential Issue Team Director, an interagency horizontal team concept borne of the new National Security Act of 2020. These new teams were a composite group of interagency players formed with greater cohesion and streamlined extra-cabinet-level authorities granted by Congress for better national mission accomplishment.

Gone were the days of lead agency peer competiveness in national missions both abroad and in the continental United States. Congress had seen the struggles of the early 21st century and decided to support the Executive Branch with greater abilities to tie all the competing departmental funding streams together with the support of an overarching select committee for national contingency missions. Kristina and her newly appointed Presidential Issue Team would form under this convention and oversight, making her the leader of the most powerful, single U.S. interagency team ever formed. She would now put this new structure to the test in the country of Pacifica, as it too, as much as Econistan had years earlier, teetered on the brink of failure and widespread instability.

I was now teacher watching student exceed my own previous level, but I also knew that some things would never change. The experiences that she and I had shared would put her in good standing for this new challenge. I hoped she would remember the core of our collective planning and execution management principles. Only time would tell.

The planning and execution management strategy was set based upon a thoughtful systems approach and a proper integration of the ends, ways and means. The time horizons of the different and sometimes competing actors from the development, diplomatic and military communities had been considered and the operations began to unfold as would be expected.

Pacifica was not Econistan, and tribal aspects were now replaced with other old but familiar struggles over power, this time between criminal elements and the supposedly legitimate forces of a fledgling, democratically-elected government.

Pacifica itself was part of an island chain that represented less of a direct U.S. national security threat to any specific concrete interest, like energy supplies, but rather it was a symbol to the region of U.S. resolve, matching strategy to its rhetoric of supporting free societies.

Kristina was clear on what the ends, ways and means were in this case. She and her staff of generalists, tied to robust reach-back support from parent agency experts back in Washington, were more than capable of understanding the nuances of the political and social landscapes.

As an old friend and sometimes mentor/consultant, I traveled out to her headquarters to see whether I could both help and learn. I was pleased when I arrived at her headquarters just at the moment she was about to go into a staff meeting – I sat in even before we had had a real chance to speak.

"I have a note from the prime minister today ...," she began.

When the meeting ended, the staff had their instructions to begin preparing for a series of joint planning sessions with the national cabinet staff on the near-, mid- and long-term strategies and priorities for ensuring national stability in the face of enormous corruption across the public and private sectors. The incidents were increasing, and the culprits seemed clearly identified, but everyone was painfully aware of the endemic nature of this particular challenge. This would not be a matter of simple border disputes, tribal peccadilloes and such that could be managed by more tangible gestures such as security and supplies. This was hard-core, embedded and almost viral corruption that had worked itself into the very marrow of the country's past, present and foreseeable future.

After the meeting, Kristina and I had our moment alone. With the door closed, she confessed to her uneasiness. No matter the challenges we had faced and experiences we had collectively, and no matter the advances we had made in concepts, structures and interagency processes since 2011, she was feeling a sense that something wasn't quite right. We both discussed this until the afternoon turned to dinnertime and her obligations were again calling. I left with a mission to ponder this conversation.

My time in Pacifica was short, unfortunately, and I departed with no full resolution of our concerns. I could tell that Kristina had welcomed the visit but was otherwise preoccupied with the enormous complexities. I knew I would not see her again until she returned to the States, but I would carry her burden with me for the next several months.

Unlike previous situations, the environment in Pacifica failed to present the usual high highs and low lows. Nothing was easy to discern or grasp on to. It began to have a feel like the U.S. 'war on drugs,' with a dubious sense of progress – and sometimes a feeling of a zero-sum game. I knew that as a person of real action, Kristina had to be frustrated.

The months faded into the second year and, while we remained in touch, the sense of unease had not lessoned, in fact it had increased. It was time to turn convention on its head. It was time for renewed analysis. What had we missed after all the years of experience and the lessons applied from the hard knocks the United States and we personally had taken? Would there ever be a time when we really got things right in our abilities to bring about the effects as intended with our friends around the world? Could we finally get an effective strategy match to our always-lofty policy intentions?

With the election of the new U.S. president, the former president's envoy was recalled and the mission came to an end, primarily based on a waning sense of whether the present course would ever yield the intended results in Pacifica, coupled to a subsequent new policy of less interest in this particular region from the new administration.

Kristina felt deflated and somewhat defeated in her own mind but was buoyed by so many who understood and thought otherwise about her and the successes, however less than expected, that she and the team had achieved. There had certainly been the aspect of proofing the concept of the Presidential Issue Team. That had been a raving success, demonstrating the efficacy of a new breed of national mission teams with real authority over funding and mission execution across the Cabinet players. That said, Kristina and I would retire to a beer from time to time to take full measure of what she/we could have done.

Two years later, we got our answer. As an island community, Pacifica had a hopelessly difficult task of maintaining all the proper relationships and coordination across the region. The criminal element had for too long begun its own 'island hopping' strategy (reminiscent of the United States' own military strategy of island hopping in the Pacific during World War II). By the time the United States had arrived, the noose had been nearly set.

Unfortunately, Kristina's interagency team had not come with a robust, functional intelligence apparatus that could properly identify and track the extent of this series of concentric rings, or network, of island corruption in the global private sector that led to a stream of supplies and financial support to the criminal elements in Pacifica. The intelligence had all been too focused on whether the neighboring governments were the carriers or supporters. Few had considered the squishier commercial aspects surrounding those island governments.

Needless to say, Pacifica suffered a coup that very next season, led by the same military the United States had helped train, but spurred by the local and, as we now understood, wider regional and even global network of criminal support and persuasion.

The geography had also played an unusual part in the equation, causing confusion as to how to link the functional area of intelligence to this vast and physically noncontiguous dimension of the problem. Taken together as a whole, these two dimensions would have provided the balanced perspective that was needed to formulate the proper strategy to meet the expectations set by national policy. Without this fully integrated functional and geographical perspective, the solutions presented never addressed the underlying causes. Said another way, the ends were never properly identified and so the ways and means were off the mark.

Kristina and I resolved to speak on these matters to whomever would listen, but I was only somewhat satiated when I received the first in what I knew would be an old and tiring string of questions from the audience on why we didn't know all this from the beginning.

<u>The Main Lesson:</u> As context in time is important, it is equally important to understand the geographical and functional dimensions of every problem. Without these contexts, missions are doomed to be reactionary, doomed to take the expedient rather than wisely considered opportunities, doomed to be shaped <u>by</u> rather than <u>to</u> shape the environment.

In our story, I had learned the following:
- Every problem has either a geographical and functional dimension or both, and both must be considered as symbiotic to the other.
- Sometimes a functional dimension such as intelligence may be seen as trans-everything (borders, cultures, etc.) and so not affected by geography. But the special aspects of our physical world also still affect every one of these.
- In today's world, and even into the future, geography still plays an important part in human interaction and also human systems integration. Even with explosions in sense making, knowledge fusion and accessibility, good ole geography matters.
- It also goes without saying, that geography alone also cannot provide all the perspectives necessary for problem identification or solution development.

Dream Sequence 8 (How it All Comes Together):

My age had ripened, but I was thoroughly enjoying the newfound respect across the Washington community generally accorded to former senior practitioners. Even without all the usual academic bona fides, I was a frequent guest professor and lecturer. I could not help, though, wondering if my time had indeed completely passed. We were on the edge of a new decade and the world was not yet rid of windmills or dragons. Perhaps I might give it one more go.

My political connections had sustained me through a wonderful network of friends whose stars had risen. I decided to have an unusual dinner with one of my best friends, and one of the brightest stars in both the Washington and, indeed, international constellations. What made it unusual was the purpose of my dinner invitation. This time, it would not just be for pleasure. I was actively pursuing an idea that perhaps I could still make a difference of a more tangible nature.

My friend delighted in my favor requested and, within a month, my own star had risen enough, with his help, to merit a meeting with both the secretary of state and the president. From there, my status was high enough for a recommendation to the United Nations for an appointment as the Special Representative of the Secretary General for Stability Affairs to the region of Africassa. Here lay in ruins the remains of several tribal, transcultural and state entities and, under this proverbial rubble, the hopes and aspirations not just of the millions of local displaced and disenfranchised, but also the genuine interests of nearly twenty countries from around the world. My task would be to makes sense of all this and recommend policies to guide a new regional strategy to address the ailments inside these challenges.

Of course, my first task came by nature, as I assembled a crew and set out on the systemic analysis of the ends, ways and means that would be necessary to accomplish our grand task. Within no time, the form of my team began to align with the functions outlined in our strategies and we were able to socialize a way ahead with all the appropriate actors. This process came with great costs in terms of compromises, as these things will when great political and social pressures push against the business-as-usual apparatuses from the often-competing sets of interests from around the international community.

My focus, however, remained steady on the people on the ground and the effects we could manage in the various and responsible time stages across the geographical and functional complexity of the challenge. There would be no 'right' strategy, as I had thought in Econistan, only a series of good-enough adaptive plans capable of evolving as necessary to synchronize the right strategies to the right evolving environmental realities.

I knew intuitively, for example, that even within a single region, a single country or a single tribal area we might be simultaneously in different stages of the overall strategy. For example, we might be simultaneously in Stage Two in the north and Stage Three in the south of a single particular country. This was the reality of the complex world, but because we understood this nature, our approach was rather simple, steady and effective, not forced.

There would be no shortages of integrated means to the ways. My staff was a nimble one. They too had their previous experiences, and contingency planning had become a matter of course. The core and surge capabilities of both our processes and structures made shifting to environmental factors relatively easy compared to my rather archaic and stultifying experiences in Econistan.

Kristina's experiences still remained close to my heart, and my admonishments to my staff to force unconventional planning and execution across the breadth of all the possible functional and geographical realities of the Africassa region gave us the tools to remain both adaptive and one step ahead of our threats. We were in the business of creating opportunities rather than reacting to threats. We were in the driver's seat. We were shaping rather than being shaped by external forces, but we never lost sight of how arrogance, confidence and even success can eventually grow into complacency and lead to blindness. We remained realistic and grounded.

I retired permanently from this wonderful, culminating experience three years later. My family and I had enjoyed our final adventures, and my successor today is still reaping the benefits of our decades of careful reflection and the years of thoughtful application of those lessons. The media has been kind in their special reports and investigative exposés of both the ongoing challenges and, more importantly, the tangible improvements in the lives of millions affected by what they dubbed the 'Africassa Dream.' As with all dreams, they can be unpredictable but, as with some, they turn out great. This dream, built on the backs of thousands of wonderful souls working hard to apply the core principles of planning and execution on behalf of others, had at last come true. It remains a dream from which I hope never to awaken.

The Main Lesson: It actually all does work. The Space, Globe, Regions and sub-regions, Countries and U.S. Internal (SGRCI) Integration Framework below is a visual representation of the seven lessons taken from the dream sequences.

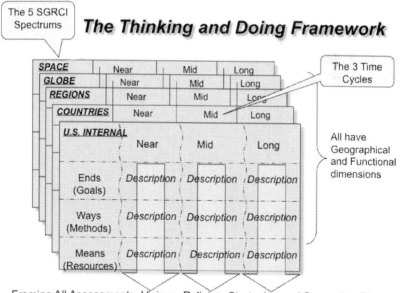

Figure 10

Here we have the lessons of the ends, ways and means integration across the multiple spectrums (more fully represented as the five SGRCI spectrums) in the near-, mid- and long-term in both geographical and functional dimensions. This framework forms the foundation of thinking and doing, or the planning and execution management, of national security.

In our final story, I had learned the following:

- There are always new and evolving circumstances, and no shortage of ideas, but the sage notion of understanding and applying the fundamentals never gets outdated.

PART VIII: THE FUTURE SYSTEM IN AN OPERATIONAL SETTING

Here is a chance to see the proposed system components working together in a future complex setting. If this works, you should be saying to yourself at the end of this, "Hey, if I were the president, I would want this planning and execution management thing."

I am going to give you one more scenario, a different one, for your enjoyment. This time, unlike the dream sequences, I am going to end with a series of testimonies from each of the future main national security actors or organizations in our scenario: the future president; the future NSC; the future Presidential Issue Team Director; the future Congress; the future Key Allies; the future country in need (Pacifica); the future NAVIC staff.

The Scenario Baseline:
1. The year is 2018.
2. The NAVIC exists fully in form and function and is housed in a building structured as stipulated.
3. The federation of information architecture is also in place and each of the receiving nodes of the various widespread actors across the private and public sectors have mini NAVICs (most often converted from Emergency Operations Centers already in place as a result of previous Department of Homeland Security directives in 2006) as stipulated at an average upgrading cost of $2.3 million each, and an annual operating cost of $1.6 million each thereafter.

4. The NAVIC is fully manned by seven teams (Secretariat and the six Planning and Execution Functions) for a total of 203 personnel, with an annual budget of $43.6 million, and performing all the tasks listed in this proposal.

5. The new president has a Senate-confirmed Director of National Security in addition to her National Security Advisor.

6. The NAVIC Executive Director is successfully in place as a political appointee and serving equally as one of two Deputy Directors of National Security. The other Deputy runs the NSC's daily business.

7. All six assistant directors of the NAVIC have been in place for six years, since the founding of the NAVIC in 2012. They are politically appointed for fifteen-year terms and have served two administrations already, one Republican and one Democrat.

8. The Office of National Intelligence has agreed to participate in full at the behest of the Director of National Security to provide the unprecedented national assessments stipulated in this proposal to the DNS and the NAVIC.

9. The NSC staff maintains constant pressure on the NAVIC to perform to their standards and to their specified needs. The NAVIC delivers without getting involved in policy decisions.

10. The NAVIC receives visits both virtually and physically by the NSC staff and Cabinet members on a daily basis.

11. The NAVIC Director attends most briefings on NAVIC output to the president by the DNS and so interacts with the president at least on a monthly basis.

12. The two main executive/legislative oversight councils are in place and have been functioning for four years, across the two different administrations since 2014.

13. The Office of Management and Budget has now altered its systems approach to synchronize its work with the NAVIC's facilitated policy and strategy development, in keeping with consolidated environmental assessments both in the near and long term. The OMB is so impressed with the NAVIC's unprecedented ability to synthesize not only the input but the outputs of expenditures on such strategies that it has moved

a significant number of its offices permanently into the NAVIC to be completely integrated with the ends, ways and means conversations.

14. The president utilizes all the reports and enforces these report development procedures across the planning and execution management of her Cabinet's work.

15. The president's Situation Room is now in perfect synch procedurally and technologically with the NAVIC.

16. The president asks for the NAVIC reports on a weekly, if not daily, basis.

17. The president visits the NAVIC facilities at least once a month for various joint visioning and policy-formulation sessions, with her key NSC staff members leading these jointly with the NAVIC professionals in assistance. The 'Think Room' is the president's favorite state-of-the-art, multi-experience room, complete with a 'Captain's Chair' approach to receiving and interacting with information in the most creative yet concise ways, unprecedented in previous times by previous presidents.

18. The NAVIC cadre of professionals includes hybrid career specialists from the National Security Professional Corps, now in its tenth year of existence. Among these are experts skilled in the art of visioning, long-range policy formulation, long-range strategy making, long-range planning support to subordinate planners, interagency capabilities master data managers, international gaming and partner integration experts, and senior generalists skilled in the art of overall facilitation and complex adaptive systems integration. None are advertised as having any particular skills in any one policy arena but all have had five to ten years, or more, of practical, hands-on experiences on the ground in foreign countries, working on matters related to national security in its broadest sense, and ten to twenty years of working in more than three departments of both domestic and foreign focus.

19. The NAVIC has links to private sector visioning and futurists from around the world, to maintain a finger on the pulse of the cutting edges of the multidisciplinary scientific communities, from the social sciences to the physical sciences.

The Walt Disney Company has two former 'Imagineers' leading programs in the NAVIC's Visioning Center. Apple, Inc., engineers accompany this team as well.

The World Futurists Society has its headquarters on the first floor of the NAVIC.

20. The president and the Executive Branch leadership have embraced all the seven principles of the new Planning and Execution Management System for national security. This includes chiefly the most inclusive view of what sectors of society are included in a national security system, defined as anything that affects the viability or vitality of the nation; the massive reforming necessary to adhere to the new fundamental core and surge behaviors across all departments and agencies; and giving the president operational authority to form composite Presidential Issue Teams operating 'above' Cabinet level with up to $5 billion in annual resources with no interference from Congress in the first year.

The Scenario: Pacifica is Going South.

On June 8, 2018, U.S. President Jennifer Landon, at the request of the President of Pacifica and with the sanction of the United Nations, signed an executive order authorizing the formation of Presidential Issue Team Alpha (PIT-A), with direct support from the U.S. State Department and the U.S. Department of Defense, to organize and lead a coalition operation to support Pacifica (a South Pacific republic). The purpose of the mission was to prevent Pacifica's fledgling democracy from falling into the hands of undesirable radical influences, thereby causing greater instability in the region.

The situation was tense, but the mission was characterized as preventive in nature because radical influences were perceived to be far from achieving a tipping point for regime change. Yet, since the installation of the new Pacifica president two years ago, economic stagnation and decline in key sectors, coupled with a recent typhoon, had the international community concerned about leading indicators for political unrest. It was agreed that this moment must be seized in order to prevent an even greater requirement for intervention in the future. This mission was named 'Operation Stable Pacifica.'

The Host Nation Situation: Pacifica was an island country in an archipelago of the south Pacific with a land area of 110,860 square kilometers, a coastline of 3,735 kilometers, a population of 11,423,952, and a Gross Domestic Product of $45.1 billion. Following a long period of authoritarian rule, two years earlier an unelected successor government seized power. Most international bodies quickly recognized this successor as a legitimate and welcome ascendant to the office.

The United States reestablished diplomatic relations and reopened its consulate after a three-year absence. All had not gone well with the fundamental changes toward a more free society.

Legacy corruption had left the public demanding faster results in the economy and other basic welfare needs, including distribution of clean water and health care. Graffiti for change had appeared throughout the country. Small pockets of radical groups had begun to show signs of organization, resistance and willingness to arm in rural areas of the country. Rhetoric from many of these groups had recently increased as resistance leaders began to infiltrate statements in the media of their willingness to resist any international intervention that would oppose the growing opposition to the new government.

Police and government military intelligence had identified 150 to 200 radical organizations throughout the countryside, but none had emerged as a dominant force. It was suspected that some may have received small arms, mortars and rockets through illicit markets. These small groups were increasingly seen as leveraging pirates and criminals to instigate instability in a demonstration to the general public that the new government could not protect their livelihoods.

Responding to increasing calls for change, the new president, Maoro Konstan, had announced his intention for elections to be held in one year. The United Nations believed that this timeframe was overly ambitious, given that the last census taken in the country was in 2000. The concern was that this could be used to fuel opposition claims of election fraud. The new president had also attempted to ameliorate the situation in other quarters by releasing some political prisoners, conducting interviews on radio and television, and announcing plans to establish a new and more independent judiciary.

Unfortunately, the new government had demonstrated its inability to handle the growing emergency forming in the countryside. As such, the President of Pacifica had asked the international community for assistance at this critical time, claiming that the "world's most recent democracy" was teetering on the brink of collapse.

The United States and other international partners had committed to offer aid to this new government and, as a consequence, had agreed to lift the sanctions imposed on the previous regime.

It was determined that the United Nations would not run this intervention. This would be led by the United States and would include operations by both military and robust civilian expertise.

Recent environmental developments had served to make matters worse. In addition to the political situation, a typhoon recently hit the eastern part of the country, cutting off sections from communication with the capital and causing severe damage to the nation's infrastructure and manufacturing base, particularly key ports and telecommunications.

As coordination began with the provisional government of Pacifica, its president identified key short-term and long-term priorities for the international donor community, as follows.

– Initial Humanitarian Assistance and Disaster Relief: Humanitarian relief and recovery along the coast as a result of the typhoon; environmental oil spill cleanup to limit damage to fishing industry; initial U.S. military support to policing matters in affected areas to prevent looting and crime; immediate importation of humanitarian related goods.

– Longer-Term Reconstruction and Stabilization: Restoration of key infrastructure and mobility corridors such as ports and telecommunications; reconstruction and stabilization assistance strengthening its fledgling market-based economy, including improved international trade and investment, intellectual property protection, commercial law development, international standards, and strengthening of its currency; assistance with elections, including conducting a national census; improvement of economic measurements to guide economic policy; U.S. civilian and military support for counterterrorism operations; limited international peacekeeping operations within its borders as a last resort, with minimal U.S. or coalition footprint on the ground; improvement of building standards along the coast to safeguard against future disasters; improvement of disaster response and prevention along the coastal region.

Pacifica's government looked like a fully functioning government with a full listing of ministries that had been in existence for many years. The actual functioning of the ministries was consistently problematic, however, in that the government was trying to move from a personality-based power structure to a parliamentary system with an official bureaucracy. The new president came from the hotel and tourism industry; he had no direct knowledge of how his government should (or could) work, beyond what one would expect from a corporate executive. The previous regime depended on power emanating from the Great Dictator; those ministries who had leadership related to or with influence over the dictator had tremendous power.

The government of Pacifica had set up an interim Ministry of International Coordination to coordinate all the Humanitarian Assistance/Disaster Relief, Restructuring and Stabilization, and donor support. The government had requested that the U.S. Mission and the Pacifica International Coalition Military Force Command would each interface and coordinate their efforts with this body.

International Situation: Other foreign governments were already working to help the government of Pacifica in its efforts to begin restructuring the economy. Key players included China, the European Union, Venezuela and Brazil. Countries with strong ties to the former regime were there as well, working to preserve their interests and to influence the direction of reform. U.N. organizations had held a presence in the country for over fifteen years and had continued to work with the U.S.-led coalition to support with its organizations as required and had already offered cooperation to USAID. Australia, the United Kingdom, Thailand and Japan had formally joined the Pacifica International Peacekeeping Force (PIPFOR) in supporting the U.S.-led coalition. Yet everyone understood this would be a U.S.-led but U.N.-sanctioned intervention.

The U.S. Government Scenario Situation and Response: In support of U.S. and international interests, the President of the United States determined that the conditions had been met to launch a whole-of-government coalition effort to lend greater support to the transitional government of Pacifica. This operation would organize under a civilian-led Task Force mission headed by a presidentially-selected Presidential Issue Team (PIT) Director from a previously Congressionally approved pool of Senior Executive civil/military, coalition-experienced Presidential Executives-at-Large. The Department of State and its U.S. Chief of Mission in Pacifica would provide the lion's share of the PIT's core in-country staff.

The following agencies would make up the PIT-A's team, complete with a robust reach-back capacity: Department of Commerce, Department of Defense, USAID, Department of Treasury, Department of Justice, Department of Transportation, Department of Agriculture, Department of Health and Human Services, Department of Energy, Department of National Intelligence, Office of Management and Budget, the General Accounting Office, Department of Homeland Security, Department of Labor, the Federal Communications Commission, the Drug Enforcement Agency, and Customs and Border Protection.

On June 8, 2018, the president directed the DNS to establish the PIT in Washington. On June 10, the president directed the DoD, Department of State and USAID to support the PIT in planning and execution of this mission in coordination with and reporting through the NAVIC. The PIT worked with the NAVIC to stand up its own internal Task Force Integrated Planning Cell, coordinating directly with the designated Pacific Regional Commissioner Headquarters (recently installed), co-located at the Geographical Combatant Commander–Pacific Command Headquarters and the Pacifica Mission, as well as other ally partners facilitated virtually from within the NAVIC.

The PIT Director used the services of the DoD to deploy his initial forward planning and execution management cell to the Regional Commissioner and Combatant Commander–Pacific Command Headquarters to assist in the development of the size and composition of the national surge requirements from the U.S. government to support the forward core interagency teams.

The PIT Director had approved both requests and plans to designate the Chief of Mission as his Deputy Director, with the senior USAID representative in-country as Principal Deputy Director. The Chief of Mission would act as the overall Host Nation Integration Director in Pacifica, ensuring that the needs of the host nation were well attended.

The PIT had completed a review of the first draft National Assessment analysis by the NAVIC. This was completed in coordination with supporting assessment personnel from the USAID Disaster Assistance Response Team and DoD Civil Affairs teams on the ground in-country as of twenty days ago. This U.S. government Strategic Plan, facilitated by the Director of National Strategy Development in the NAVIC, was based on this analysis as articulated in the subsequent Policy Advisory Memo dated June 30, 2018. As a result of the NAVIC analysis, the PIT-A Integrated Planning Cell recommended the deployment of its advance party to link up with these assessment teams on the ground.

From his forward location, the Chief of Mission began drafting his subordinate Interagency Implementation Plan for Pacifica based on four major Lines of Action – Justice and Security; Governance and Participation; Economic Stability, Infrastructure, Humanitarian Assistance and Social Well-Being; and Public Affairs – with the initial priority on short-term Humanitarian Assistance/Disaster Relief and then longer-term Restructuring and Stabilization operations. The Chief of Mission utilized the mini-NAVIC-in-a-box technologies brought in by the PIT quartering party to tap into all the national NAVIC planning support capacities, including national assessments, policy formulation analysis, red teaming, gaming, and planning experts. Two of the quarter party members were, in fact, civil/military plans and operations experts brought in to assist the Chief of Mission in facilitating and setting up his own planning and execution management cell.

The operation took place in three broad phases. Phase I: Initial Response; Phase II: Transformation; and Phase III: Fostering Sustainability. The U.S. government conducted operations in each of these phases through the following four 'Lines of Action.'

Security and Justice (Tasks for the former include disposition of armed and other security forces; intelligence services and belligerents; territorial security; public order and safety; protection of indigenous individuals, infrastructure and institutions; protection of reconstruction and stabilization personnel and institutions; security coordination. Tasks for the latter include interim criminal justice system; indigenous police; judicial personnel and infrastructure; property; legal system reform; human rights; corrections; community rebuilding; anti-corruption).

Governance and Participation (Tasks include executive authority; legislative strengthening; local governance; transparency and anti-corruption; participation; census and elections; political parties; civil society and media).

Economic Stability, Humanitarian Assistance, Infrastructure and Social Well-Being (Tasks include refugees and internally displaced persons; food security; shelter and non-food relief; public health; education; social protection; employment generation; monetary policy; fiscal policy and governance; general economic policy; financial sector; debt; trade; market economy; legal and regulatory reform; agricultural development; social safety net; infrastructure; transportation; telecommunications; energy; and general infrastructure).

Public Communications (Tasks include print; radio; multimedia; local organizations; transparency; support to government legitimacy; economic transformation; and elections).

Each of these Lines of Action was assigned to a PIT Core Team to both plan and implement at the strategic and operational/tactical levels of implementation. The teams would have both forward and rear components and both would use the services of the NAVIC to assist with planning the strategic shaping.

International Military Mission: As lead of the Pacifica International Peacekeeping Force, the U.S. military will initially conduct support for humanitarian assistance and disaster relief operations in Pacifica in order to alleviate human suffering and to assist the government of Pacifica in maintaining legitimacy.

In support of Reconstruction and Stabilization, the Pacifica International Peacekeeping Force will conduct Foreign Internal Development or support training and development of internal security sector forces and ministries, as well as conduct and support United Nations forces in counterterrorism security operations to assist the government of Pacifica in developing and maintaining immediate and long-term stability. It was hoped that this may help set the conditions necessary to support free and uninterrupted elections at some future date. To date, the Pacifica International Peacekeeping Force consists of forces from Australia, the United Kingdom, Thailand and Japan, but would welcome and was actively recruiting other neighboring country contributions as well.

PART IX: HOW THE MISSION UNFOLDED UNDER THE NEW NATIONAL SECURITY PLANNING AND EXECUTION MANAGEMENT SYSTEM OF 2018 AS SEEN THROUGH THE EYES OF ITS KEY PLAYERS

From the perspective of U.S. President Jennifer Landon: I entered the Think Room of the NAVIC with my accompanying NSC staff and Cabinet members for the deliberation 'experience' orchestrated by the DNS. The NAVIC had its work cut out for it. By the end of the 90-minute session, the NSC staff and key Cabinet members, with assisting NAVIC professionals, presented me with all the essential fused aspects of the environment affecting Pacifica and its potential for success or failure. The presentation went according to the usual script using the now-venerated ends, ways and means integration SGRCI framework enshrined in National Security Doctrinal Publication NSP-1, version 2.0. The situation in Pacifica was only one of the eighty-five high priority issue areas being managed by the NAVIC across the five environmental spectrums.

To be exact, upon taking office, I had approved planning and monitoring of thirteen issues for Space, twenty-two issues affecting the entire Globe, seven Regional issues affecting a total of thirty-one countries and seventy-two percent of the Earth's population, seventeen

Country-specific issues, and twenty-six issues of national security affecting the Internal U.S. mainland. I was intimately familiar with this framework model, as the reports I received daily from the DNS and my Cabinet were always broken down into these same categories, and as I sat in my captain's chair, I was able to ask very penetrating questions about Pacifica after the briefing had ended.

Furthermore, because my staff and the NAVIC were already fully integrated with the resource management arm of my executive branch, and also because my team had fully integrated the Congressional oversight and watchdog councils high and early, I could, at that very moment, turn to my team in the Think Room to get a strong sense of whether the Pacifica situation was spinning out of control and, if so, what I had at my disposal to do about it.

The NAVIC's risk assessment modeling plus its red teaming of the NSC staff's preliminary recommendations on Pacifica gave me a good feel for the complexities and the potential tradeoffs. All of this was displayed visually in front of me, and this conversation was beaming real-time to all the participating actors' mini NAVICs around the globe with two-way, full-sized 3-D, Blu-ray surround sound quality.

I saw the impact of doing nothing clearly from the presentation 'experience' that the Visioning Team had brought forth. After my staff and I took our multisensory headsets off, we clearly understood in the most visceral, four-dimensional way that the United States' presence on the ground in Pacifica would change lives. This multisensory briefing technique had prepared me exceptionally well, combined with the series of ten eight-minute visual presentations in addition to my twenty-minute pre-presentation discussion I'd had over coffee with my inner team of advisors in an adjacent room just minutes before joining the full staff in the Think Room.

I thanked the DNS for orchestrating this fine staff work and mentioned that I was particularly happy with the work that the NAVIC had done in pulling together the experience. I left the room to join my advisors back in the adjacent President's Room to discuss the options in more detail. I understood the integration factors for my national ways and means to support my ends, and I understood how this particular matter of Pacifica fit inside the context of my administration's broader Grand Strategy priorities based on my National Security Review and the status of the government and commercial systems at play from our ongoing (living) National Operational Analyses. My national assessment teams had helped me link my original priorities to the evolving environmental factors of red (key adversaries), blue (key U.S. missions and program outcomes) and green (key partner intents, missions, programs and capabilities affecting this issue area) across all the various spectrums, and I knew how they all were leading me toward change in both the near, mid and long term.

I was confident that no matter the direction, my executive branch was more ready than ever, after a five-year reform effort had finally produced a more modular executive branch with core and surge templates for easy reconfiguration to respond to any national or international need. I had already experienced success with my first Presidential Issue Team a year earlier, with its whole-of-government execution of a mission in the homeland during an earthquake in central Missouri. I also knew from that experience that the 'living' quality of my planning and execution management system and products were the key to a flexible response, especially when some of the preconceived plans had been off the mark.

I felt gratitude to those who had the foresight in previous decades to see these visions for a more effective 21st century national security planning and execution management system and, in this particular instance, I could feel the way ahead. But now I just needed a bit of time to soak it all in. A decision would be forthcoming in the morning.

From the perspective of the NSC key staff and DNS: We had been through this before. Many of us had served in a previous administration during the last decade before the NAVIC even existed. At that time, each staff member spent all their efforts trying to be both a strategic policy and plans specialist and an advisor to the president. When the shift came to expand this role with an added responsibility of ensuring that the executive branch was following these policies and plans to the president's required conclusions across the breadth of interagency actions, each tiny two-to-three-person office in the NSC became completely overwhelmed.

But the real shocker came when the media lambasted the previous administration for not thinking strategically beyond a few months and in repeatedly fouling up the legislative agenda with incoherent priorities across an undisciplined and near-term politically expedient set of issues, while long-term perspectives continued to fall through the cracks. No one in the NSC staff had been able to cope. The system just had too much to respond to.

The myriad of actors in the system were also often working at cross purposes because no common understanding of national principles in planning and execution management existed – archaic structures were the rule of the day – and a multitude of different stovepiped niche issues each with their own corresponding niche procedures and frameworks that only the individual creators understood made the increasingly complex world impossible to keep up with. Yet that was now all in the past.

Today's presentation experience on Pacifica came on the tail of years of reform and reeducation of an entire cadre of national security professionals, and it was clear that both the president and the wider staff were better for it. Specifically, from our perspective, and because the NAVIC provided the thankless tasks of synthesizing and presenting our policy positions with the best available information on Pacifica at our direction, we were better able to zero in on the necessary policy pieces that still needed the president's help and approval. By having the NAVIC work on Pacifica in the background, we were freed to consult with our own experts and partnering agencies to build an even better portfolio.

Moreover, because the NAVIC housed real planning experts with the time to think the big thoughts and with a lifetime of expertise from across the many sectors, the rotating political NSC staff didn't have to rely on doing something it neither had the time nor skill sets to do by itself. We learned to trust the people in the NAVIC, as they truly had no political agenda. None were administration political appointees and all had a sense of continuity from previous experiences that proved invaluable through the chaos of presidential transition in the previous year.

On the second front of helping the president manage the overall execution process of the national security system and, in this case, Pacifica, we could back off and let the Cabinet and the NAVIC worry about that. This again freed us to stay focused on our advisory roles to the president.

Finally, the NAVIC had given all of us in the NSC and DNS a neutral home for integration, and it paid huge dividends prior to the presentation on Pacifica. Before the NAVIC, we met periodically in normal meeting formats clustered in the Old Executive Office building with limited meeting rooms. Sometimes we simply met in the hallways. Now the NAVIC is our dedicated source for integration and, as their charted chief client, all our requests are treated with utmost priority.

The facilities of the NAVIC have also forever changed and advanced our ability to both collaborate within the NSC and across the agencies, and to plan with both great creativity and in ways we had never expected or previously been exposed to. The Old Executive Office Building simply wasn't designed ergonomically to facilitate such 21st century integration. The NAVIC's neutral facilitation also helped ease the inevitable interoffice politics and occasional infighting that can ensue under great stress even in the best of organizations.

Finally, the overall system of integration of the national ways and means with the ends that the NSC proposed to the president was a complete and radical shift from the days when one section spoke with the Office of Management and Budget while most of us had little clue and, therefore, little effect on how the Office of Management and Budget or Congress helped us resource our goals. Now, the NAVIC provides this facilitation under one roof on a subject that was often far too complex and fraught with bureaucratic cultural differences between those more concerned with only counting dollar signs and those of us measuring the success of our programs on the ground.

For Pacifica, with the inclusion of the legislative oversight mechanisms through a neural platform such as the NAVIC, it became a win-win situation for both sides. Transparency has increased trust without violating any of the president's prerogatives or violating the sanctity of the president's political maneuvering on the Hill. The natural inclination has been to trust these oversight mechanisms and to make them work because they came to represent unprecedented access to the executive branch for Congress - an opportunity it never wants to pass up. Consequently, the best and brightest junior and mid-career office holders in both legislative bodies staffed these oversight councils in the new system.

Today, to serve on these councils has become a plum position and is considered a steppingstone to even more senior positions inside Congress because of the access it provides these members to the president and the experience gained in executive branch operations. So, from our perspective on Pacifica, we were equally thrilled that Congress cared and gave us an essentially nonpartisan, third-party platform for our issues, concerns and requests to support our recommendations to the president. Nothing is perfect, but so far both sides are winning.

From the perspective of the key Cabinet Secretaries: The Founding Fathers would be proud. This great country continues to reinvent itself without compromising even a punctuation mark in the Constitution's venerable principles and tradition-setting precepts.

At first, many of us were concerned by what we perceived as a threat to our individual department agendas and the power of our Cabinet status to move the president, when necessary, toward our agendas. The introduction of the NAVIC and the National Planning and Execution Management System in 2012, with its Presidential Issues Teams and such, was considered a direct threat. While on paper we remained a working Cabinet in the great traditions of our forefathers, in practice we perceived an infringement on the total sovereignty we had enjoyed for over two hundred years.

That said, everything about today, in the year 2018, and using this issue on Pacifica as an example, has made new believers out of us all. The tremendous advantages gained by the nation over the modest losses we experienced in our rather smallish departmental perspectives have been more than worth any sacrifice. To be clear, we really have lost nothing. We still remain the backbone of the executive branch and, in that sense, the only 'doing' arm of the administration. We are also still the president's chief advisors on all things departmental. We are appointed by her and have her ear any time we need it. We simply now find ourselves more as equals among our peers than perhaps we may have liked to think of ourselves before.

By this we mean that the president now has a much more balanced and complete perspective of the risks and tradeoffs across the entire interagency. Before we could not do justice to either the complexity of the cross-agency integration issues or to the simple solutions we might recommend. The Cabinet meeting room and the president's meeting format, with its tired old briefing highlights, was simply no match for the real world need for planning together.

The old solution for us was to resort to all manner of informal tactics to get our way, and almost all of these tactics were at the expense of collaboration. Said another way, because there was no formal system in place for the president and us to interact in planning rather than broadcast meetings, we all resorted to 'insurgency tactics' to get what we needed for our individual departments. And the NSC staff was powerless to stop us.

The NAVIC and the new Planning and Execution Management System changed all this by adding just enough formality to the process to bring us together without trouncing completely on top of us with a bureaucratic and wasteful centralization of the agenda. It took a few years to work out the kinks, but we have arrived at a good place and the horizons look bright. The NAVIC, in particular, has been a great asset, and we have members of our team on their team. We all gain. The NAVIC's skill sets beget our own and vice versa.

The overall Planning and Execution Management System has also proven time and again to be a complement to our agenda, not a competitor, because it gives us greater access to others through common shared information architectures and superb ergonomics when the need arises to meet in person. In the case of Pacifica, at the behest of the NSC and the DNS, our respective staffs met on the NAVIC premises three times prior to the presentation experience with the president. All of these meetings were constructive and all of the deliberations were instantly and transparently available online as we returned to our offices, making internal dissemination and decision-making inside our individual department levels a cinch.

The System also increased the quality of our time with the president by leveraging the NAVIC's expert abilities and facilities to game our policy stances before we met with her. By the time of the Pacifica presentation, we were certain about our recommendations because we had actually gamed them out like the DoD – something we could never have conceived of only ten years earlier. This System really helped the domestic agencies in particular because it let them compete on the same playing field with the likes of the DoD and its decades of experience in ends, ways and means integration.

Finally, it was difficult, but now that we have mastered the rudimentary aspects of the national doctrine of core and surge, even the domestic agencies no longer tremble at the notion of contingency operations. We get it. If we have to give up just a bit of our department sovereignty to the Presidential Issue Teams, it is a small price to pay for the much greater overall good to the nation. We are comfortably behind the PIT-A and its cross-agency leadership role in Pacifica.

From the perspective of Congress: The implementation of the new National Security Planning and Execution Management System has been a rousing success. Both the Infrastructure and Manufacturing Oversight Council and the Ends, Ways and Means Integration Oversight

Council have given the legislature unprecedented access to the daily decision-making of the president. The spirit behind this alone has made a huge difference in traditional executive/legislative relationships, and both of these councils played an important role in the lead-up to the Pacifica situation.

Because of the change in paradigms from supporting an executive branch with only a few expeditionary members to a full-up, whole-of-government expeditionary capability, we in the Congress have had to be prepared, with our venerable committee structures, to be as adaptable and flexible as the departments are now. The new core and surge ethos has translated into real processes and structure adaptations that our forefathers could never have dreamed of. The world has simply become too complex and dynamic, and the time element of responses too important to leave to the old, bureaucratic legislative processes of the 19th century. We had to adapt, and adapt we did.

In 2012, we adopted changes to our committee processes to streamline them for a 21st and 22nd century ends, ways and means integration institution to match the new executive branch paradigm shift. We all approved this, but the going was very difficult. We haven't yet achieved all the necessary adjustments but, with Pacifica, we were able to take many first steps in showing off our ability to be flexible, timely and adaptable.

The National Infrastructure and Manufacturing Oversight Council, in particular, was our first, and perhaps still most unsung, adaptation. Infrastructure and manufacturing management doesn't exactly stir the imagination but, as we learned from the DoD, there can be no overlooking the future requirements across the entirety of the U.S. government. Before, we were all content to let the DoD set the example on this. Today, our country would be in peril if we had not taken the steps to force not only the rest of the executive to get out in front of its future requirements but for us to do the same.

U.S. infrastructure and manufacturing base is the backbone of the means to any national end. If we don't have a cutting-edge national capability, we can't offer a cutting-edge response to the next Pacifica.

But because we've begun to recognize the magnitude of this challenge, we have all set in motion a national infrastructure and manufacturing management program that will not only affect future Pacificas, but will affect the health of our own nation at large, including the jobs associated with such national capabilities.

The new National Security Planning and Execution Management System gave us this opportunity by creating this council to bring us together seamlessly and continuously with the executive branch in a neutral setting. We put our best and brightest young House and Senate members on this council to both give them executive experience and to bring the energy needed to this critical function. Pacifica is now benefitting from this because the president and we have a clear-eyed strategy to match the 10-, 25- and 50-year Presidential Visions of national infrastructure and manufacturing capacity to respond to any contingency. Perhaps we will be remembered as a visionary generation, because we saw and met the horizon with our ideas and our actions.

The National Ends, Ways and Means Integration Oversight Council has also been essential for us to merge the big think with the more pragmatic, as our Constitutional mandate requires us to. The National Ends, Ways and Means Integration Oversight Council gives us an operational insight into what is needed and how we can play the most constructive role in helping meet these needs with our two branches. Again, we have stocked this Council with our best and brightest.

Bottom line: As we walked into the joint presentation experience with the president on Pacifica, there was no daylight between us all. We were on the same team.

<u>From the perspective of the Presidential Issue Team:</u> As the Director of PIT-A, I saw firsthand the impact of the new National Security Planning and Execution Management System leading up to the events regarding Pacifica. I had previously served as both a Presidential Czar for U.S. domestic planning and execution of the nation's global warming initiative and as an Envoy to the country of Econistan when it too was

struggling to remain stable. In both cases, I can easily say there was no comparison with the capabilities I enjoy today with the new system.

Previously, I could have only dreamed of true planning and execution management across agencies. Back then, I never had the power to be operational. If I wanted to be operational, it would have been based on a myriad of compromises, cajoling and, in the end, little real power. If I asked for more power to bring coherency and unity of purpose and action under one roof, I was met with legal obstacles and infighting among the various constituencies both in the executive and legislative branches. Agendas ran deep and politics even deeper, and the mission, and most importantly the people on the ground, suffered the most for it. If being operational is defined bluntly as being able to put funds directly to an intended action with no interference, I was far from being operational. I never had the ability to match funds to the actions my staff and I, nor even the president, deemed essential without months of wrangling all manner of entrenched bureaucratic and political challenges. Today, that has all changed.

With the advent of the National Infrastructure and Manufacturing Oversight Council and the Ends, Ways and Means Integration Oversight Council, Congress understands and feels less threatened by the nature of the executive requirements and, more importantly, feels it has a true say in the president's agenda on national security. These councils have been instrumental in bringing both branches closer together, but it was a tough fight getting us there.

Today, I am benefitting from the foresight and action of both these councils. My team was ready and well resourced for the mission in Pacifica and, most importantly, Congress trusted the president, and by extension me, with the immediate contingency funds and the authority to use them as I pleased with no strings attached for the first year. We will be wise with our use of resources because we want to demonstrate to Congress that this was not a measure given in vain.

My mission in Pacifica began without so much as a hitch across the entire interagency when it came to funding and supporting my mission with the people and resources I needed in a timely fashion. No longer was the DoD the only entity in the entire government capable of such massive planning and execution management at a moment's notice.

Yet, I can't go a moment more without mentioning perhaps the most important aspect of all this, which gets little attention these days. The core and surge paradigm shift of the entire U.S. government has given the United States the single greatest edge in our global reach to help others around the world and to protect our interests. By adopting this model and adapting it to the civilian world in both process and structure, and combining this with the new cadre of civilian leadership now coming of age from the initial days of the National Security Professional Corps, begun in 2006, the U.S. government is truly a modern phenomenon.

While we once feared the rise of other mega-powers on the world stage, such as China, we ended up on the leading edge of the route to supremacy because we changed the rules of the game rather than continued playing the same old game. Instead of trying to compete simply with brute force, we got smart with the application of our capabilities. Instead of leading primarily or only with our Department of Defense, we created a national capability to lead from any direction, in any direction, when and how it was necessary, with the full might of all our instruments of influence, at a moment's notice.

We changed our rules of interaction and collaboration, and that changed the entire global equation. Now, China is not only years behind our capabilities and spending massively to keep up, it is light years away from, and perhaps may never truly match, our nimbleness because of its sheer size.

So, as Pacifica is today, so will it be in the next crisis. We will respond with precision and move quickly in and out with a comprehensive approach while others try to match with brute force, as we tried to do at the end of the 20th century and the beginning of this century. My mission is going quite well. The NAVIC continues to provide me the wherewithal I need across the continuum of U.S. interagency collaboration back in Washington and, indeed, across the nation. My team forward is able to quickly seize opportunities when they see them simply because they are finally now truly operational. We are making great progress.

<u>From the perspective of Pacifica:</u> As Director of the newly established Ministry of International Cooperation in Pacifica, I have been mostly concerned with the operations of PIT-A and the U.S. Embassy, but I have kept up somewhat with the changes in America. Who hasn't? It has been quite remarkable really.

We are a small nation and have become quite adept at dealing with great powers. It is a survival quality that all small nations must possess if they are to exist at all. But it is rare for a great power to also think like a small nation. By this I mean to understand the essential qualities of doing the most with what you have. Great powers are not used to worrying about this. The United States, however, has begun to see the world this way, and this has made a major impact on the globe.

Today, the United States understands it can no longer compete with resources alone. It must compete with skill and precise action. To do this, it tackled its own demons, unleashed by decades of being on top and wanting to stay there. The economic collapse of the earlier decade helped America see itself in a new way – not as a sole and omnipotent power on a mountaintop, but as a savvy explorer looking for ways to add value, learn new things, cooperate with the environment and, yes, those of us around the globe. They not only began to think like this but, capitalizing on what the rest of us have most admired about America and its people, they did something about it.

There is no doubt PIT-A and its ability to add value to our little country is but a small yet tangible example of this new America. We in Pacifica know America cannot remain here to help us forever. But we also know that America now comes with both a new spirit and tangible methods of cooperation. This new America gets things done even better than before because it comes as a total package without the political baggage of the home front infighting we used to watch on television, especially between the Departments of State and Defense.

Moreover, we are now meeting so many more U.S. government representatives from previously obscure agencies. We have seen a great deal of change in the skill and capabilities of other U.S. agencies, and even the USAID is now complemented by the fullest extent of U.S. official government-to-governmental agency relationships that last a lifetime. We also no longer meet the United States first through its military. We are grateful for these and all the other changes in the American system.

From the perspective of Key Allies: America has never been more effective at any time in its entire history than it is today. From east to west, we have watched with amazement as the United States turned itself into a well-oiled and balanced machine of state without giving up its characteristic maverick and pioneering qualities that inspired us all for two centuries.

To be allowed inside the tent, so to speak, with the NAVIC facilitation during the runup to the Pacifica mission stood as a singular example of the shift in American attitudes and practical approaches to the rest of us. For almost the last seventy years, and increasingly so in the last twenty, the American government, with its think tank shadow republic in Washington, grew into a nearly unrecognizable series of centers of power and influence. None of us could discern from year to year exactly how and where to interface with the States to get things done. The planning and execution of its national government had become so diffuse and distributed that we used to joke privately that perhaps global warming would be good because it would flood Washington and make them start all over. Thank goodness it didn't take such drastic events.

The National Security Planning and Execution Management System is now the model many of us are wishing to import. We see tangible evidence of the greater speed and efficiency of U.S. government operations from what they were only a decade ago. Just when we all thought there was nothing new under the sun, America did it again.

In Pacifica, we are part of their PIT-A under the auspices of the United Nations. We now know how to work both the forward and rear integration and collaboration with the U.S. government. We understand the entry points into their decision-making processes because they now know them themselves. The president has become more than a mere political head of government and is now an actual head of government because she 'commands' her executive branch better than many of us thought possible outside of parliamentary systems or dictatorships.

America is still experimenting with its own democracy, and this latest experiment has given all of us a new vision of the possibilities of executive and legislative cooperation, as well as of its effectiveness. We are most impressed by America's visioning, and its helping bring coherence to what we can all do together to shape a better world beyond merely the immediate.

From the perspective of the NAVIC: The six assistant directors have been working at full tilt, and Pacifica is only one of many factors in play. Today we presented to the president on Pacifica, but we are moving toward nine more presentations next month on different issue areas.

That said, we couldn't be more pleased with the way this all turned out only six years after we completed our pilot. The six assistant directors have now experienced two different presidents and we, as a team, have begun to prove two of our most advertised selling points – that we are nonpartisan and that we bring a critical and neutral continuity to the planning and execution of national security.

Many were skeptical, but we proved all the critics wrong. Today's presentation experience was just the same as with the last president on similar issues. Our systems are truly color-blind, and the results show in the amount of participation we get from both political parties. We also proved our worth to our most valued customers - the NSC staff and the subordinate players under their influence. Never before had the NSC staff been able to multiply the breadth, quality and timeliness of their services advising the president as they can today.

We work in the background with our world-class talent. We bring perspectives from around the world and from any sector to the NSC staff. The 'thinking' side of the national security system has never been richer. As for the 'doing' side of the equation, we continue to build on our experiences, but if Congress's General Accounting Office and Congressional Budget Office are any measure, the reviews are in and they couldn't be better. We have proven our ability to help bring the planning of national security full circle into connection with the execution through the management of all the flow of products and services between and among the various actors all under one roof (physically and virtually).

Our staff, with our informational architecture, has been able to make the 'living' quality of all of this a reality. We have become the perfect complement to the government core and surge paradigm, providing cutting-edge services at a moment's notice because we can draw upon our vast reservoir of data and experience across the various administrations.

Our third-party location and neutral status has given us the perfect physical and political positioning to do what the NSC alone could not do in decades past. Finally, our early and high integration of both the advocates and the watchdogs of the government under this same 'roof' has brought a quality of transparency and trust that is now exemplified in the resulting Pacifica mission portfolio.

We are eagerly learning as we go along with our National Operational Analysis team and we hope to continue adapting to the requirements of the NSC and our wider interagency customer base with these and other services as they may need.

PART X: WHY DEPARTMENTS MATTER TO NATIONAL LEVEL REFORMS

After all is said in this proposal, I would be extremely remiss if I didn't speak to a critical part of this paradigm shift that either doesn't register with most folks in Washington or is at the very least simply taken for granted. I've decided to devote an entire section to this to make the emphasis complete.

For too long, Washington, D.C., has operated with a false assumption when it comes to national security matters, both at home and abroad, namely that people alone equals capacity. The belief is that if the government simply gives every agency more people, every agency will be able to participate in any national mission with great competence. This is simply not the case. Capacity equals people plus all the other issues we've been talking about in this book: structure, process, resources, etc. In the end, if the national security system expects to have a competency in national planning and execution management, it will sink or sail by whether there is an equal and parallel planning and execution management capacity at the subordinate levels – for all practical purposes, a thought lost on most of Washington.

Consider the latest progressive idea floating around Washington in one niche sector of national security, the sector of nation building (or as insider bureaucrats like to call it, Reconstruction and Stabilization – but try to sell that in Peoria). In the wake of Iraq, the United States government created an office to work this issue across the 'whole of government.' Unfortunately, this new office was placed in the bureaucracy below the Cabinet level. This office (the Coordinator for Reconstruction and Stabilization) was placed in the bowels of the Department of State and was charged to build collaboration across all the other departments in the executive branch. Everyone could sense that this wouldn't work, but the experiment went forward anyway. Now we finally have a proposal, some many years later, by the Iraq Reconstruction Inspector General that maybe it's time to move this office up to a place above the peer Cabinet level so it can really start getting things done. Just one small problem – it is still a completely flawed vision.

This latest proposal, like nearly all others in the capital, remains focused on the creation of a national level solution but with no mention of or effort dedicated to building the parallel capacity in the subordinate levels to truly empower this national concept. Every single national concept is only as good as the subordinate capacity to support that national concept. Quite frankly, I don't have the answer for why this myopia continues, but it does.

In Washington parlance, the phrase 'whole of government' refers to the notion that support to national missions and programs requires every part of the government putting its oars into the water. This is a great evolution from the previous days when no one really placed an emphasis on this. Some are now calling for whole-of-nation approaches, and I have called for whole-of-globe approaches to national security as our futures continue to intertwine around the world. But, as I have made the case, we have to do more with these slogans.

So this leads to the conclusion (keeping the discussion to the interactions just within and amongst the U.S. government for now) that for every national level reform, there must be an equal and corresponding reform at the department level. Said another way, no matter the national reform, nothing will get done until the departments have the equal capacity to participate and keep up with the latest 'good idea.' This lack of foresight continues to plague all the best of intentions. The result has been a litany of unfunded mandates dumped on top of the already beleaguered departments. Therefore, every good idea at the national level (including those in this book) must also come with a corresponding capacity building package with funding at the department level.

The '3Ds' (defense, diplomacy, development) has been used to describe the so-called pillars of U.S. national security since it was coined in the 2006 version of the U.S. National Security Strategy. The 3Ds are embodied in the Department of Defense, the Department of State, and the U.S. Agency for International Development. These are still seen by most as the only pillars of national security because, until recently, no one considered the true breadth and depth of national security issues and how the entire executive branch (and the nation) can and must contribute to them.

Recently, however, the '4th D,' a phrase describing the rest of the executive branch, has crept into the discussion around town. (This phrase was coined by me and my Department of Commerce colleague Merriam Mashatt in our 2008 article, "Domestic Agencies in Reconstruction and Stabilization: the 4th D," published by the U.S. Institute of Peace.) It is not popularly known that the 4th D is actually comprised of a multitude of departments, agencies, boards, commissions and programs in the following functional categories.

Agriculture
Business and Commerce
Community Development
Consumer Protection
Cultural Affairs
Disaster Prevention and Relief
Education
Employment, Labor, and Training
Energy
Environmental Quality
Food and Nutrition
Health
Housing
Income Security and Social Services
Information and Statistics
Law, Justice and Legal Services
Natural Resources
Regional Development
Science and Technology
Transportation

Each of these national functions is further delineated into over 170 subcategories that make up the rest of the executive branch and, in my mind at least, the real whole-of-government and its national security capacity. To the untrained eye, this may not look like a Who's Who list of national security areas but, when considering any national mission, from assisting New Orleans to assisting Kabul or Phuket, each of these functional categories is ripe with talent from across the executive branch ready to assist this or any nation with getting to its feet in peace time or before and after an emergency. If one thinks about it, none of the 3Ds (defense, diplomacy, development) knows what it takes to keep a nation running, but the U.S. domestic agencies do it every day. This capacity must be nurtured, cultivated, developed and released into the larger national security community to make its contributions. Without it, there can be no 'whole' in the much-ballyhooed phrase 'whole of government.'

To be fair, the State Department and a few others have, over the past several years, broken ground in creating some 4th D civilian working groups to address a few national security issues, mainly in Reconstruction and Stabilization (or nation building), but this new civilian capacity could and should be extended to apply to any national mission, both foreign and domestic. The State Department, with its foreign-only mandate, however, is mostly focused on leading a recent Congressional effort to fund the creation and maintenance of a particular civilian reserve corps designed to deploy a first tier of deployers to reconstruction and stabilization missions within forty-eight hours and a second tier within thirty days. These civilians are the beginnings of a new national security capacity in the domestic agencies whose efforts should be applauded. Unlike contractors, this new government reserve has the potential to add unique value, at least in the reconstruction and stabilization arena, with the following contributions.

<u>Long-term government-to-government relationship building (impossible with contractors)</u>: The 4th D provides specialized ministerial-level expertise for the nation in need. Government

officials possess unique skills in helping to build capacity related to inherently governmental matters. Most importantly, however, nations in need respect and view as a sign of U.S. resolve the exchange of such ministerial level government advisement.

<u>Reach-back to a robust and functionally aligned stateside home base capacity:</u> Reach-back (calling back by phone or Web-based communications) to home base support is a relationship between two teams – one small team conducting business forward in the field and the stateside home base team (usually in Washington) that supports the deployed team with answers to its questions and resource needs. The intent is to establish a seamless virtual relationship between the two that, while separated by thousands of miles, leverages a dual approach and enhances performance in the country in need.

Reach-back to a home base adds great value by taking the burden off the very small forward team in the field to coordinate complex whole-of-department coordination from thousands of miles away. The home base can, for example, conduct this complex coordination while the forward team keeps working on other issues. The home base team can then send out the results of the whole-of-department coordination a few days or hours later to the deployed representatives for consideration.

<u>Domestic agencies have significant untapped potential with their close ties to the private commercial sector, including:</u> Helping the private sector to navigate regulations and laws encountered while doing business overseas. Working with in-country national, state and local officials to reduce barriers to private sector trade and investment. Helping the U.S. private sector develop mutually beneficial partnerships with companies, civil society organizations and government bodies in the country in need to address sensitive political and public policy issues and to invest in practical projects.

<u>Promoting activities such as:</u> Advocacy for good governance and anti-corruption measures; developing voluntary codes of corporate

conduct; creating innovative public-private financing mechanisms for health, education, civic institution building and infrastructure and manufacturing development; and facilitating corporate donations.

In My View...

National level and Department level Capacities, both forward deployed and in the home base, have to be considered <u>equally</u> as two halves of a whole in order to make 'whole of government' more than a slogan.

Figure 11

Recognizing the gap in domestic agency capacity to contribute to a national security call to action, pilot programs have begun. One in particular, under the auspices of the Institute of Defense Analyses, could catalyze a growth in the necessary 4th D capacity over the next several years. As the chief consultant in this IDA program, inspired by my Department of Commerce colleagues Merriam Mashatt and Jay Brandes, I am working with leaders in several agencies now to create simple, basic departmental capacities in both planning and execution management in the home base supporting its deployed personnel that could apply to any national mission, either foreign or domestic.

My approach has been a bit revolutionary for a couple of reasons. First, my approach has been to finally get away from the years of

Washington creating specialized niche frameworks to plan and execute different mission areas such as counterterrorism, nation building, global warming, ... you name it. This only serves to confuse and overwhelm the departments. They can't keep up with all the different planning and execution frameworks for every issue area, but that is what they are being asked to do. Just take a look at the scope of the problem facing the departments by glancing at the chart below. Everyone wants a piece of them.

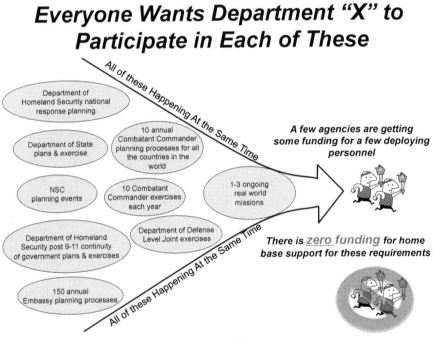

Figure 12

The 3Ds all want representatives from department X, Y or Z at their planning and execution meetings, programs and missions. Moreover, they each have their own unique business practices and often these are different for each issue area. The departments just can't keep up, and how can we blame them?

My approach alleviates this because it is based, yet again, on a critical assumption that for me has become a fact. I say this based on my experience in the management of both planning and execution of large, complex team missions. This critical assumption is that planning is planning and execution is execution, no matter what the mission profile. By this I mean the informational inputs and outcomes may be different but the general formula for how to think and do complex profiles remains generally constant. The processes are all essentially the same. There are no real differences worth speaking of, but instead of seeing the commonalities, we have proliferated methods of discontinuity and competing frameworks. It is simply crazy, and a recipe for continued confusion and disharmony.

As I have made the case already, the complex future must not be met with greater complexity but with greater sophistication in our simplicity. No more niche frameworks. We need to proliferate a general set of skill sets in planning and execution management that can handle any national mission or issue area thrown at it. In my own case, and in the case of others I know, I would be as comfortable in a commercial boardroom as in a military headquarters or the NSC when it comes to planning and execution management. They each offer a different challenge requiring a great deal of learning about the inputs and desired outcomes, but the process of thinking through all this is entirely similar. This approach is what we need to be developing in our government. We need common approaches across our entire breadth and depth of composition so that we can face the array of complex problems as a team.

My second revolutionary component of this work at the department level is that I am not worried about what all the other reformers do in this town, because what we are doing at the department level is designed to be basic enough to fit into whatever national level frameworks are finally adopted. Our approach at the department level will ensure that each will be the very best partner in ANY national process of planning and execution (including my own proposal, if adopted). Why do I believe this? Because I know what national level planning and execution management teams want from a participant. I have directed such teams, and all I ever wanted, or could hope to expect, is that each participating department or agency knew what it brought to the table and how to employ it. As the Oracle of Delphi stated so many thousands of years ago, the most important thing to know is thy self. This is true of departments as well as individuals. If every department has an internal process to know itself, it will be a superb partner in any national planning and execution process. My approach to building this same capacity in each of the departments is to create just such an effect. Each is different, and so building this planning and execution management capacity in each department requires a tailored approach, led by the folks in that department. The only thing that remains the same for each is the end goal. So far, it has been very successful and, in my mind, the beginning of a modular approach to the national thinking and doing.

This isn't about 3Ds versus the 4th D. All of the Ds need each other for national missions to succeed, and the development of these capabilities must be a two-way street. For both sides to gain, each has to help the other move towards the requisite skill sets and capabilities that constitute a true whole-of-government capacity.

To reemphasize, the future of U.S. national security requires the ability to put the full talent and might of its whole of government to bear on the problems abroad as it does domestically when called. But in order to do this, the paradigm has to shift from the idea of deploying individuals to deploying departments as a national capability. In terms of changing the reform game, I offer the following suggestions.

- Think in terms of trained domestic departments, not trained personnel.
- Understand that funding a forward reserve corps misses funding the all-important home base capability to stand behind these few.
- Equate the 'forward' personnel of a department to the tip of an iceberg and the 'home base' as the portion underwater in order to fully appreciate the message of capacity building in the domestic departments.
- Create the additional funding and the legal mandates (with authorizations to spend money) from Congressional committees for

each department to build, staff and maintain a permanent national mission home base planning and execution management capacity.

- Understand that this core capacity resident within each domestic department will not only benefit the departments but will finally allow for the realization of the true meaning behind the hollow rhetoric of 'whole of government' echoing still from the last decade.

- Eliminate niche frameworks for national security thinking and doing tailored to each different mission profile.

One of the great ironies of the 4th D movement may be that through its emerging initiatives, visions and insights it may actually provide the venerable 3Ds with an example of cooperation and synergy still not fully achieved in their own ranks.

That said, none of this has any inevitability to it. The challenges are great and the way ahead is clearly uphill. It will take visionaries from across the U.S. government to make the case for real, deep and systemic change in both the executive and legislative branches in order to realize a true national security capacity.

PART XI: CONCLUSION. WHAT MAKES THIS PROPOSAL "BETTER"?

Here, I must finally reveal the compelling case for why all this is better than what we have now. So many more threats and opportunities exist over the horizon, but it would be impossible to game them all in this or any book. Certainly, nothing can be taken away from any of the successes of this or any future or past administration, Democrat, Republican or Independent. So it is my burden to demonstrate why such successes might not be all that they seem and why improvements are still needed. That task might be best summed up in the question: Why is this proposal better?

To address this fundamental and critical question, which underpins the entire premise of this book, we must first deal with the question of what qualities or criteria a national security system of planning and execution management should have as a standard against which to measure 'betterness.' Following this, one would have to somehow quantify those criteria on a measurable scale. Finally, one might then be able to compare and contrast the system of today to the system I propose in this book.

Let's start with a list of what I propose are the qualities or standards (metrics, if you like) that any national security planning and execution management system ought to achieve in order to be considered complete and competent. (Notice I did not say 'good.' That is a value judgment to be determined later by you. Right now, we must remain objectively focused on unbiased standards.) Some might prefer that

I describe standards for a system that would be feasible, suitable and acceptable: feasible in that it is in the realm of the possible; suitable in that it addresses the problem; and acceptable in that the system participants would all agree to it. Pick your going-in lens. I think the following system standards are a good start and may serve as criteria for assessing 'betterness.'

<u>System Standards for 'Betterness'</u>
1. Holistic: The system treats Planning and Execution as two halves of the same coin with no daylight between them at any level.
2. Tangible Outcomes: The system produces tangible outcomes largely for people on the front lines, not processes or organizations and not for the bureaucracy all along the way.
3. Timely Outcomes: The system produces outcomes in a timely manner and eliminates time-wasting process steps both in steady state and, especially, during crisis.
4. Prevents System Overload: The system handles multiple crises at once without missing a beat and every participant is fully informed with no confusion.
5. Operational in Crisis: The system allows the executive branch to match funds more directly to action (and is therefore fully operational) during crisis for reasonable periods of time with nearly zero intermediary steps, while submitting to streamlined, 21st century oversight mechanisms from Congress on behalf of the American taxpayer.
6. Measureable: All outcomes are measureable and the system measures these in a quick and comprehensive manner.
7. Learning: The system ruthlessly learns from its outcomes and quickly makes adjustments.
8. Stewardship: The system eliminates financial waste.
9. Anti-Corruption: The system eliminates opportunities for fraud and corruption, both at home and abroad.
10. Efficient: The system is efficient in that decisions produce results with as few intermediary steps as possible.

11. Provides Continuity: The system remains effective and efficient regardless of passing leadership or political affiliation and during all transitions.

12. Inclusive: The system produces solutions that represent all points of view from inside and outside the usual insiders crowd of influencers. All actors (including subordinates) feel included and not excluded in the option development, functions and, most importantly, outcomes of the system.

13. Realistic Decision-Making: The system provides the president and all system participants with both a formal and informal process of decision-making. The formal allows everyone to participate and be heard. The informal allows for the prerogatives of key leaders and natural tendencies for insider reflection.

14. Handles Complexity: The system never slows for complexity. The system makes complexity seem simpler to everyone involved.

15. Nimble: The system is extraordinarily nimble in both planning and execution of policy and strategy.

16. Contextual: The system provides future contexts to all nearer-term choices.

17. Provides Options: The system provides options to all decision-makers at all the various levels.

18. Supports Subordinates: The national system is matched with, and is only as good as, the equal planning and execution capacities resident in every subordinate system.

19. Creative: Nontraditional actors are involved in decision-making high and early for greater overall perspective and creativity.

20. Policy/Strategy Matching: The system ensures a Policy/Strategy match for each End.

21. Integrates Ends, Ways and Means: The system ensures every Way is supported equally with the Means, and they both clearly support a particular End in a manner that every single actor understands and supports.

22. Maintains Presidential Prerogatives: The system does not interfere with presidential prerogatives but, in fact, enhances these.

23. Sustains Informal System: The system does not interfere with the informal political system of decision influencing but, in fact, enhances this.

24. All-Seeing: The president 'sees' the entire system and all its actors in complete ways and always in the proper complete contexts of both time and space.

25. Steady in the Boat: The system can function fine during any attack on the homeland, including a weapon of mass destruction.

26. Disseminates Common Picture: The Knowledge Management architecture enhances all these qualities listed here as a first priority in both planning and execution.

27. Prepares the Human Equation: The Human Capital architecture matches the system requirements, especially its nimbleness in planning and execution.

28. Fills in the Seams: The system resolves current, and prevents future, development of strategic 'seams' in both planning and execution of national security that could be exploited by adversaries.

29. Broadest Perspective on National Security: The system treats the concept of national security as holistically as possible, measuring itself against the one main standard of addressing anything that can affect the viability or vitality of the nation.

30. Anticipates, not Reacts: The system anticipates and resolves tension, conflict and complexity before any become a crisis.

31. Open, not Closed: The system is an open system so that it can grow and reflect the world as it is and not as the actors inside closed circles would wish it to be.

32. Shapes, not Shaped: The system shapes the environment in which it interacts more than is shaped by it.

33. Americans more Involved: American citizens more clearly understand their government's work in national security and are able to see their government at work online without the filter of media bias (similar to C-SPAN), and so feel more connected to their democracy than ever before.

34. Adheres to Fundamentals: Finally, every 'attribute' and 'imperative' listed in this book are inherent in the operating system of planning and execution.

I leave it to you to decide whether the existing formal and informal systems are as efficient as what I am proposing. I would invite you to scan or reread sections of this book with the standards listed above now in mind. You decide which is better. I chose not to give you my own position for each, as they will undoubtedly be biased, but also because I do not wish to inadvertently influence your own creative process and analysis.

I will offer only a couple of guiding thoughts as you reflect. Planning and Execution Management is more than a policy design tool. It is more than a strategy-making tool. It is more than an operations tool. It is more than a subordinate planning tool. It is more than an operational analysis, tracking or assessment tool. It is the sum of these parts, and more, when the intangibles of morale, teaming, creating opportunity, building trust, applying vision and foresight, achieving effectiveness of outcome, and so much more are also outputs of a system like this working as a whole.

Finally, as you compare and contrast your own experiences, or those of others, to this proposal, please recognize the inherent difficulty in observing the world around us in the required depth for a true and accurate analysis. What may seem simple on the surface may in fact be complex beneath what you see. What may seem quick may have taken years of preparation. What may seem efficient to you may not be from another functional perspective. What may seem transparent may be obfuscated to others. What may seem anything from one system perspective may seem quite different from another perspective within that same system. So, before we are to crown the existing system either broken or good enough, we owe it to ourselves and our successors to attain a real understanding of what is in front of us.

PART XII: AN ILLUSTRATIVE PROPOSAL TO THE PRESIDENT

What would a national planning and execution management proposal be without a plan of action to bring about these changes? In the interest of sparking ideas, but not in prescriptively presenting a solution, I offer an example approach for creating a national planning and execution management capacity in four stages that would likely take place over the course of several years. These stages are:

Stage 1 - Evolution and socialization of the problems and potential draft solutions.
Stage 2 - Finalizing, approving and socialization of final solutions.
Stage 3 - Implementation of pilots.
Stage 4 - Learning and adjusting from initial results of implementation.

Some details are in order.

Stage 1 – Evolution and Socialization of the Problems and Potential Draft Solutions: I have stressed from the beginning that the ideas presented in this volume are not final nor are they necessarily complete. I have offered these thoughts to start the debate at a point farther down the road from where I believe the current national conversation resides. I hope that these ideas will bring forward even better ideas in keeping with the spirit of what I propose. That said, the first stage of any attempt to actually build towards this new national capacity must begin with a series of steps designed to evolve our thinking together as a community, perhaps with my proposal as only a starting point. To do this I would argue for the following.

Step 1A: Establishment of the Presidential Commission for the Planning and Execution Management System of the 21st Century. This would begin with a public announcement by the president. A Presidential Study Directive would follow appointing an Executive Director and a Deputy Executive Director to recruit three Discovery Directors who would then develop a charter and manage the commission programs, all working for the Director of National Security.

The charter would include:

- A statement of the national security planning and execution management problems and their causes as outlined in this book (there is a great deal of recent literature out there on this topic to help out). Academic institutions, rather than agenda-ridden Beltway think tanks, could assist.

- A working hypothesis of a future national security system based on the thoughts expressed in this book with its foundational principles, clearly stated assumptions, a description of overall desired behavior for the parts and the whole of a new national security planning and execution management system, and specific expectations of performance outcomes and effects on key audiences for the system at each of the various system output points. This working hypothesis would only be a point of departure for the commission participants as a way to jump-start the team effort instead of starting everyone from a blank sheet of paper or waiting to do an exhaustive literature review of the problems and causes. A good enough approach will do. The emphasis of this commission approach will be on active, hands-on, give and take, experimental discovery processes rather than research.

- In addition to the hypothesis, the commission team would also propose a core statement of the Commission's purpose, scope, structure, methods and descriptions of expected outcomes and success over time.

- Finally, the charter would include a terms of reference appendix outlining proposed milestones for an implementation plan.

Step 1B: Following this, a very small expert team of seven persons would be hired around each of the three Discovery Directors, each aligned to a different function of the overall system and the NAVIC itself:

National Assessments, National Policy Making, National Strategy Making, National Support to Planning, National Support to Implementation, National Operational Analysis, NAVIC Structure, Processes, Resources and Systems Management, Additionally, each Discovery Director would receive an additional three supporting staff members for administrative management.

Step 1C: Unlike most commissions, this Commission would be conducted in a styled competition of ideas between the three composite discovery teams formed in parallel to review, analyze, propose, and experiment with the starting system hypothesis across all of the six functional areas and the NAVIC. Each of these three teams will open all meetings to all congressional staffs but will specifically receive two permanent liaisons by direction of the House and Senate Majority Leaders – one each from the Government Reform Committees of the House and Senate assigned for no less than two years. These discovery teams would conduct all their work out of offices provided to the Executive Office of the president with congressional funding administered from the Senate Government Reform Committee for a five-year program at the National Defense University. Again, academic institutions from across the east, west, south, north, and central United States, rather than Beltway contractors or think tanks, will provide the additional staff secondments, as requested, to these teams at the urging of the president.

The three teams would adhere to the intent of the charter for overall guidance but would be encouraged to produce clear and distinct choices on the content of their proposals and counterproposals for the six functions and the NAVIC for presidential consideration. These choices could be variations on the initially proposed purpose, scope, principles and performance outcome expectations for a new national security planning and execution management system or something radically different. In other words, all new ideas would be welcome.

Step 1D: With a commission structure in place, the Director of National Security would convene a small group (only six to eight) of key senior mentors from both the executive and legislative branches, including sitting leadership of the National Governors Association, to formally assist, starting with approving the Commission's charter. The senior mentors would also assist the Director of National Security in reviewing all the final work of the discovery teams.

Step 1E: The three discovery teams would embark on a process of discovering the feasibility (can it work?), suitability (does it fit the problem?), and acceptability (will the system be accepted or rejected by the actors?) of the going-in hypothesis. This may include some research but the teams will be encouraged to organize and explore the going-in hypothesis through its own gaming, 'murder board' and review sessions, and practical experimentation with notable experts across the widest spectrum of opinion in order to form and draw its own conclusions. All conclusions on feasibility will then be addressed in recommendations for mitigation, improvement, or elimination and replacement. This step could take over a year to complete.

Step 1F: After the results of the discovery teams are in, and with initial approval from the Director of National Security, and to build toward an even greater consensus, the three parallel discovery teams would hit the road together to present their separate findings and justifications for recommended solutions at various speaking engagements across Washington, various universities around the nation and to the media over a six-to-twelve-month period, all heralded by the president in a national speech. Simultaneously, the NSC would direct these three teams to conduct more private joint presentations to various members of Congress and staff on Capitol Hill and in the executive branch. Here, a local think tank or federally funded research and development center, with a special legal analysis team attached, would accompany all presentations around the country and in Washington and follow up with notes on the comments and questions raised in the presentations and trend analysis for the discovery teams, senior mentor team and the Director of National Security to review.

The final stage would be a series of public hearings by the Senate and House Government Reform Committees on the various aspects of the team draft findings and option recommendations, with side-by-side comparisons on the nature of the problems and proposed solutions. Hearings will be important to begin the process of building goodwill and securing eventual funding for piloting and institutionalizing any new capacities in the executive branch, such as the NAVIC. The results of all the above would be briefed to the president and his staff for reaction and guidance.

Stage 2 – Finalizing, Approving and Socialization of Final Solutions: After the hearings are completed on the nature of the problems, causes and the potential solution sets in the first years, and the president is satisfied that the results are heading in the right direction, the Commission will move to this next stage of the program.

Step 2A: Large-Scale Gaming. The president will have decided on a general direction from the three composite options presented, but the details at the level of implementation and second order effects of those details on the overall system will likely still be uncertain. This next step, called 'gaming,' would attempt to identify these issues through a series of free-play exercises in which each of the three discovery teams' recommendations across the six functions (or others) of the proposed system and the NAVIC would be tested against varying degrees of current and future national security scenarios using people and computers to role-play different tasks of the system. An analogy of the system might be the human body, into which a dye is injected into the bloodstream. From this injection, one can see how all the parts of the system, from the heart and lungs to the brain, react. The same is true in gaming, in which a scenario is 'injected' into all three teams' planning and execution management system proposals to see how each of their parts reacts. From this, one may gain insights for adjustments.

The three discovery teams themselves would provide the role-playing of their proposed system processes while the same local think tank or federally funded research and development center in Washington, working for the Executive Director, would provide: the game design; the red, blue, and green scenario injections to stress the system; lead individual player preparation sessions; and lead group rehearsals. It may be necessary for a separate section of a completely different think tank or federally funded research and development center to conduct the observation and synthesis of the games' outcomes in order to keep the games and the gaming analysis clean and free of influence and bias. Specialized legal, human capital and knowledge management analysis teams will supplement the think tank observation and synthesis teams in observation of all the games.

The NAVIC, of course, would be role-played in each of these games to learn about its overall role of cross-functional integration, including the necessary boundaries of these roles.

Additionally, users or customers of the national security planning and execution management system, such as the NSC, the Cabinet, Presidential Issue Teams, and the state governments, would provide authentic members to role-play in order to fully stress the functional system designs.

All games initially will be speedy, generally low-tech for participants, and all players co-located within sight of each other in the same conference center at first – simple tabletop exercises with no extensive computer or communications equipment interface or support. The games will progress to more distributed and computer-supported events as personal skill sets, technical capabilities, and organizational procedures evolve and become more familiar to the participants. The three gaming processes may take many months to complete if done in parallel. If done sequentially, it could take over a year.

Step 2B: Finalizing solution recommendations based on results of the gaming. Here, the think tank observation and synthesis team, led by the Commission Executive Director, would work with the Director of National Security on presenting the final gamed solution recommendations to the various constituencies for concluding comments and ultimate approval. This may initiate new rounds of virtual presentations both in and out of government across Washington and the country as necessary.

This step will culminate with a second and final set of hearings and joint executive/legislative conferences on finalizing and mitigating any legal or other substantive obstacles before moving forward with the creation of legislative and executive documents for approval of a completed system for piloting. This step will take months.

Step 2C: Presidential signing of all final solutions into executive and/or legislative authoritative documents as approved for piloting.

Stage 3: Implementation of Pilots. Following the approval stage, the real work must begin. The implementation stage is a multi-year, multi-stage process involving all aspects of the six functions and the NAVIC across the multiple actors involved. It should include, as a minimum:

a) An initial and far-reaching education program to socialize all aspects of the proposed pilot systems to each of the expected participants at both the leader and staff levels.

b) Training programs following the education programs to provide hands-on experiences with the new systems (more low-tech tabletop exercises).

c) Continued research and development by an NSC-directed and legislatively approved and funded (up to $50 million for five years) office to conduct and manage pilot implementation programs in each of the six functional areas and the NAVIC with differing technical and process solutions over a four-year program.

d) Recruitment and contracting of all manner of personnel, services and equipment to bring the piloted systems to life.

e) The establishment of an ongoing joint executive/legislative implementation oversight committee to review pilot progress and eliminate waste, fraud and other bureaucratic and/or political obstacles to implementation across the U.S. government and other nongovernment sectors, as well as to develop new solutions sets or modifications, as necessary, for the president's approval. This committee will recommend which pilots should be converted into permanent programs.

f) A media outreach campaign to keep the issues transparent, online and open to criticism and learning.

g) The construction of the NAVIC functions in a pilot structure over a four-year period.

h) Finally, ongoing national games (at least every two years) to test and modify behaviors; processes; outputs, including products as well as resource needs in equipment; personnel; and funding.

Stage 4 – Annual learning and adjusting from initial results of pilot implementation must be a priority, with a culmination of the total results in year five: As an extension of the process steps listed in Stage 3, learning and adjusting will be a never-ending process but cannot happen without formal procedures put in place. As the NAVIC stands up, it will eventually house the National Operational Analysis Center that can pick up these duties to monitor the lessons learned across the system and provide recommendations for improvements or modifications. Ultimately, the joint executive/legislative implementation oversight committee will make recommendations to the president on what pilot programs should receive sustained funding as a permanent part of the new national security system.

FINAL THOUGHTS

I have laid out my best attempt at a holistic National Security Planning and Execution Management System, but I am sure I've missed something. I hope so. Exemplifying one of the many imperatives of this or any system, I am open to better ways.

This book attempts to create a broad understanding of how a president and his or her participating members might better manage the planning and execution of national security with just enough detail to make it come alive. I hope to reach a broad audience of current and future agents of change to stir a wider debate. My spirit of service and a belief that no one has yet presented anything as holistic for these times (and those to come) spurred this attempt. Finally, my ideas were in no way meant to be critical or arrogant, only helpful.

I look forward to hearing from each of you with your own thoughts regarding the matters presented here.

END